BLACK BASEBALL *in Alabama*

BLACK BASEBALL *in Alabama*

Rough Diamonds of Dixie

Shane J. Earnest, "Dr. Miraculous" of
the *Montgomery Baseball Blog*

Published by The History Press
An imprint of Arcadia Publishing
Charleston, SC
www.historypress.com

First published 2026

Manufactured in the United States

ISBN 9781467170338

Library of Congress Control Number: 2025948403

CONTENTS

ACKNOWLEDGEMENTS

It is my pleasure to thank my wonderful partner, Michelle, for her love and support during all our adventures. I thank my parents—my father, who shared fabulous stories of baseball's past, and my mother, who opened my world with books. Also, my immigrant great-grandmother, who taught me how important baseball is to those who learn it as outsiders.

This work could not have happened without the assistance and encouragement of many, including but not limited to: Bill Plot, Clarence Watkins, Jeb Stewart and the Friends of Rickwood Field, Ryan Blocker and the staff at the Alabama State Department of Archives & History, University of California–Los Angeles, Alabama State University, the Selma Public Library, the Negro Southern League Museum, the late Michael "Coach" Coleman, Ozzie Timmons, Gary Redus, Billy Gardner Jr., Brady Williams, R.C. Lichtenstein, Jim Tocco, Cameron Seitzer, Dalton Moats, Tyler Zombro, Brett Sullivan, Sam McWilliams, Jaime Schultz, Brent Leach, Chris Coleman and Anthony Overs of the Canberra Cavalry, Dr. Meredith Wills, Michael and Kristin Harders, Michael Robinson, Dr. Layton Revel, David Barath, Richard Chamberlain, Jo Chern, Rachel Corsini, the late Dr. Kate Shuster, Jeff Perro, and the kindness of all the wonderful pals at the #chilltent.

INTRODUCTION

My father played stickball in the streets of Minneapolis as a kid. One spring, they had to start in the mornings because their best player had an afternoon job playing centerfield for the Minneapolis Millers. His name was Willie Mays. Dad told me all about Willie and other Negro League greats, such as Willie's Minneapolis teammates Ray Dandridge and Dave Barnhill and, of course, the legendary Satchel Paige. It fascinated me, this alternate, hidden baseball world. Dad tried to explain why they weren't in the Major Leagues, sparking many more questions.

How did this hidden baseball world produce so many great players who were shunned from white diamonds and cut off from the top levels of the game? How could they develop their skills without the benefit of major-league coaching? How did this alternate baseball universe exist without organized leagues? The answer was simple. They *did* have all of those things, years before many white teams even picked up a bat.

Seeking to learn more, I found little information available, often recycled myths or flat-out lies. Worse yet, outside of Birmingham, no one in Alabama appeared to be stewarding the rich history of these amazing men and women. Their wonderful stories were not being preserved—they were being lost forever.

With no one caretaking this orphaned history, I vowed to do my best. I began by learning my locals, studying everything I could find about baseball in the state. For twenty years, I collected info and stories, blogging my journey as "Dr. Miraculous." I discovered that Negro League connections stretched across Alabama and far beyond, deeply intertwined with life outside of baseball.

Research for this work ranged far and wide over decades, so brevity requires much omission on important subjects. Some sources are nebulous. I have made every effort to identify the players wherever possible. Errors have surely been made, as there is much more to be discovered.

There were many unexpected events and characters, whether famous, infamous, or obscure. They were politicians, musicians, bootleggers, preachers, teachers, heroes, and villains alike. It is my sincere hope that this book encourages further discussion and helps lend a voice to those who are unable to tell their stories themselves.

Your Dr. Miraculous,
SHANE EARNEST

CHAPTER 1

PENNANTS, UNIFORMS, AND ROAD TRIPS

Following the Civil War, baseball became iconically American, symbolic of freedom and equality. Every player goes to bat for themselves, given a chance to overcome whatever is thrown at them, embodying the hopeful optimism of the country and its people. Between 1865 and 1900, Americans were introduced to the new sport as it began its rapid infusion into the country's cultural identity. As the South transformed from wartime to Reconstruction and beyond, the game of baseball swept the nation, and in Alabama, people of all races and genders welcomed a new national pastime.

One of baseball's attractions was networking. Utilizing improved roads and rail travel, baseball provided a group event for people with different backgrounds to gather on equal social standing. Baseball also made use of some of Alabama's most abundant resources, beautiful weather, plentiful open spaces, and communities with strong social bonds.

In these formative years, baseball opened a path in athletics largely unavailable to previous generations. These men and women would take to the new sport in droves over the century to come, becoming legends of the game. In time, Mobile produced immortals, Birmingham became an iconic location, and Montgomery would rise and fall. But first, the game was being learned in nearly every cotton field, cow pasture, and vacant lot in the state.

Early southern newspapers included scant information, often with racist language. However, it wasn't long before Black baseball was described with respect even in the columns of white-run Alabama newspapers such as the *Birmingham News* and the *Montgomery Advertiser*. Many places were reluctant

Montgomery, Alabama, in the 1870s. *Alabama Department of Archives and History.*

to spill newsprint ink on Black interests, leaving history largely reliant on these two cities to reflect the development of baseball in the Black communities of Alabama.

While there are no records for those who played, there are clues as to how the game was learned by Alabama's African American and forced-immigrant African population. Stories of plantation slave ballgames are anecdotal and largely considered tall tales. However, Mobile played baseball before the Civil War, and the *Independent American* of Troy published game rules as early as 1856.

Following the war, newspapers reported that Montgomery's first ballgames (1867–68) were well attended by the Black population, who took great interest in learning the rules of the game. An 1870 exhibition series by the white New York Mutuals at the state fair in Montgomery attracted many diverse fans. These games served as instruction courses for aspiring "baseballists" statewide and are often considered the genesis of baseball in central Alabama.

1871: Montgomery Blues

In 1871, the *Montgomery Advertiser* featured one of the first mentions of a Black baseball event in Alabama. It discussed, in derogatory terms, a team brandishing a pennant declaring them to be the Independent National Blues, parading to nearby Mount Moriah for a game. The Independent National Blues are among the earliest known nonwhite teams in the state. While the article mocked the Montgomery Blues, parades and postgame galas were a tradition everyone was very familiar with. Parades were popular networking tools for everything from political marches to volunteer fire brigades.

Montgomery's Court Square in the 1880s. *Alabama Department of Archives and History.*

JAMES ALSTON

Parading with the Montgomery Blues was Jim Alston. A formerly enslaved shoemaker and musician, James H. Alston became Macon County's state representative in 1868. He was victimized by repeated political attacks, including a rigged bribery scandal and an assassination attempt by the Ku Klux Klan that left him wounded but unmoved in his determination as a politician.

Alston's musical abilities were beyond reproach. During the Civil War, he was purchased in a Montgomery slave sale for $1,800 ($54,000 in modern terms) to be a drummer for the Tuskegee Light Infantry of the Third Alabama Infantry. The literate, self-taught gentleman was described

The 1872 Alabama Reconstruction Legislators team photo includes James Alston and Johnathon W. Jones, both closely involved with baseball teams. *Alabama Department of Archives and History.*

as "a valuable servant" by regiment commander (and owner) General Cullen Battle. Jim Alston was likely present at historic events such as Antietam, Fredericksburg, Gettysburg, and the Confederate surrender at Appomattox, gaining insight into the upper levels of political negotiations that would serve him well.

Respected by the community for his honesty as a politician, James Alston is honored, along with other Black members of the Reconstruction-era Alabama legislature, with a plaque on the Alabama Capitol grounds.

SELMA JOINS THE GAME

Baseball was being learned across Alabama, and Selma refused to be left behind. The *Selma Times* commented in 1871 that baseball fever in that city "extended to the lads of all ages and colors. Every vacant lot is crowded with baseballists indulging in the 'national game.'" Montgomery visited them that June for a game. In 1872, Selma's Lone Star and Atlantic clubs challenged each other, and soon many teams traveled to oppose them at their field near the old brewery. In September, Selma hosted Rome (Georgia) in a day filled with music, dancing, and amusements.

MONTGOMERY'S RAPIER CLUB

Members of Montgomery's Rapier Club were noted for their bright new uniforms in 1874. The club was named for James Rapier, the Florence, Alabama–born politician who was a leading voice for African Americans and was elected to the U.S. House of Representatives in 1872. In '74, James Rapier was running for reelection and assisted with the U.S. Civil Rights Act. It's unknown if Rapier himself was connected with the team or if his name was chosen for its political connotations.

Visually striking on the field, the Rapier Club uniform also sent a political message. Their red ball cap with a red star and a blue button set the team apart from a popular white Montgomery team that sported a similar red star on a white hat. Blue socks with red stripes added a distinct Union look to the Rapier uniforms, which likely included dark pants and long-sleeved flannel shirts.

Baseball equipment was a new commodity, and players placed orders via mail or shopped at local stores. Balls, bats, and uniforms (gloves would not be in fashion until the 1890s) were flying off the shelves at shops more accustomed to livery, fishing gear, and dry goods. Sometimes local baseball clubs offer used equipment for sale. Woodworkers and wheelwrights became bat makers almost overnight to fill the demand, and one Alabama retailer reported that it moved more than five thousand baseball bats in six months.

Baseballs.

Dead Red..$1 50
New York Regulation........................ 1 00
Practice 75
Boys' size.................... 15c. 25c. and 50

BASE BALL BATS,

25c., 50c , 75c., 85c., and $1 00.
Prize (silver) ball and (enameled) bat $8 50
Score Books ....10c., 25c., and 50
Rules for 1874.................................. 10

Clubs sending money with order for base ball goods, may

DEDUCT TEN PER CENT,

from above prices. Address

Boyd's Bookstore

SELMA, ALABAMA.

Above: Downtown Selma in the 1890s. *Selma Public Library.*

Right: Vintage caps advertisement features star caps like Montgomery's Rapier club wore. *From the 1888 Spalding's Official Base Ball Guide/Library of Congress.*

Opposite: Baseball gear quickly became popular across the state, such as in this 1874 advertisement in the *Selma Times Argus.*

1870s Across Alabama Baseball Spreads Like Wildfire

Players banded together across the state—in nearly every city, town, and crossroads—to form teams. Newspapers struggled to keep up with the volume of baseball news.

Huntsville's team rode a train to nearby Florence in 1874, one of the earliest mentions of Black baseball clubs in northern Alabama.

In 1877, a July game was held in Demopolis between clubs representing Alabama and Mississippi; Alabama was victorious. The area had been hosting games between Black teams for years, as the *Marengo News* had sarcastically reported in 1874 that the Demopolis Moonlights players were Democrats.

Athens, Alabama, boasted an excellent team called the Star Base Ball Club in the early 1870s. The club was led by L.T. McLin as team captain. Huntsville's team visited Athens in 1877, arriving in horse-drawn wagons. The Athens Stars defeated Huntsville, and reports said that the Stars were unbeaten since their inception, which occurred sometime prior to 1874. Madison, Alabama, sent its club to challenge Athens that same summer, led by captain Dennis Fletcher, but were trounced 41–7.

Opelika formed its first team around 1878; Greenville soon followed, as did Evergreen. Even tiny Claiborne fielded a team. Formerly a major shipping location on the Alabama River, the once-thriving city was decimated by pre–Civil War epidemics and postwar looting. Bypassed by railroads, its population dwindled to fewer than two hundred residents. Nonetheless, Claiborne put together a baseball team for 1879.

1800s Origins in Birmingham and Mobile

Birmingham

Birmingham got a late start compared to other Alabama cities, yet its well-planned beginnings quickly gave the town a broad base of hardworking citizens. Founded in 1871 and powered by the Industrial Revolution, Birmingham soon became an attractive destination for those seeking opportunities. By the 1880s, Birmingham had become a major producer of coal, iron, and steel. The young city was a hub for railroads, with nonwhites forming more than half of the city's workforce.

Birmingham's first Black baseball clubs were organized between the city's founding and the mid-1880s, but their existences were mostly undocumented. Teams often represented a neighborhood, mining camp, or business or had social or political associations. The Birmingham Unions were an early club with a name chosen to highlight support for worker unionization.

Baseball revolved around Birmingham's industrial expansion; teams of mill and mine employees soon organized into competitive leagues. The Birmingham Industrial League launched many careers in baseball for players of all races and were particularly beneficial for player development. Although it was a segregated semipro league, many earned more in the Industrial League than they would with traveling teams. Others, winding down their playing careers, enjoyed transitioning into jobs with pensions.

The 1891 Birmingham Hornets boasted an unbeaten record against as many as ten cities.

In 1897, the Birmingham Unions were members of the Southern Colored League. The Unions club was founded by Robert L. Jackson, one of Birmingham's top Black entrepreneurs who ran a popular tailoring business, was active in civic causes, and was considered one of the most prominent men in Alabama.

In 1904, Charles Isham Taylor and brothers Ben, John, and Jim arrived in Birmingham. Together, they founded the Birmingham Giants, instantly one of the most powerful ball teams in the South. The Giants' success helped propel the city toward becoming a premier Black baseball destination.

The American Cast Iron Pipe Company (ACIPCO) fielded a powerhouse team, winning more than fourteen Industrial League championships, including nine consecutive titles. ACIPCO games sometimes drew up to ten thousand fans during the team's heyday.

Birmingham's natural coal and iron deposits quickly made it an industrial center. *Library of Congress/public domain.*

Arthur Coar reportedly organized the Ensley Mill team in 1915. Coar, a widely respected butler at the TCI mill dining room, also organized the steel mill's white league. Ensley's steel mill would go on to field many successful teams in the Industrial League.

Mobile

One of the oldest cities in the country, Mobile was founded in 1702 as a French port. During the Civil War, it was a vital supply hub for the Confederacy and remains an international shipping center today.

In 1858, Nemesio Guillo and his brother Ernesto, along with Enrique Porto, were students at nearby Spring Hill College. In 1864, they returned to their home country of Cuba. They took with them bats, balls, and the rules of baseball, introducing the entire Cuban nation to the game. People around Mobile such as the Nemesio brothers were enjoying baseball considerably earlier than most of the country. Unfortunately, it was a period of mostly undocumented Black baseball history in Mobile. Yet there were sporadic reports offering a few details that strongly suggest that the city's multiple clubs were active and very popular.

Mobile sent a team to Mississippi in 1885, losing to Meridian, 22–12. A second game against New Orleans that afternoon was rained out according to the *Memphis Avalanche*.

The Memphis Eclipse visited Mobile for a June game as part of their 1887 southern tour.

Mobile visited Pensacola as early as 1889, and in 1894, Mobile hosted Pensacola at Frascati's Park baseball field, at the end of Conception Street on Mobile Bay. The game was a big one, attracting a crowd of more than one thousand spectators, who saw Mobile win 11–6.

In October 1894, the two top clubs of Mobile faced each other. The Alabamas and the Mobiles held a championship game in Pensacola with nearly one thousand fans watching. The Alabamas won the first two of five games, as reported by the *New Orleans Times Picayune*.

The two cities have vastly different origins. Mobile was founded thirty years before the birth of George Washington, and Birmingham was established five years after the death of Abraham Lincoln. One was playing ball before the Civil War and the other didn't swing a bat until Reconstruction, yet both these Alabama cities made immeasurable contributions to history through Black baseball.

Mobile, Alabama, circa 1900. *Author's collection.*

From Mobile sprang Satchel Paige and Hank Aaron, arguably baseball's most legendary pitcher and its most prolific power hitter, respectively. They head a long list of Negro League greats, Major League All-Stars and baseball Hall of Famers from the Mobile area. Birmingham brought forth Willie Mays, possibly the greatest all-around baseball player in history, and the city itself became home to one of the most fabled franchises in the game with the Black Barons and their iconic ballpark, Rickwood Field.

Birmingham, representing the New South, and Old South Mobile shared a sparsely recorded Black baseball history, yet both contributed immensely to transforming baseball in Alabama, across the country, and around the world.

CHAPTER 2

1880s

Baseball Firemen

A game between Montgomery and Selma was part of the annual fireman's picnic in Selma, hosted by Central City Hook and Ladder No. 2 in June 1885. Black volunteer fire brigades were integral parts of city infrastructure and sparked deep civic pride. That downtown Montgomery still has structures standing from the antebellum era is largely a testament to the Montgomery Grey Eagles volunteer fire brigade. Comprising African American and

Montgomery's Grey Eagles Fire Brigade, seen in front among the firefighters parade in Court Square in 1869, were closely connected with baseball. *Alabama Department of Archives and History.*

forced-immigrant African volunteers, the Grey Eagles were on the scene in 1865 as Union troops took Montgomery, with retreating Confederates lighting the city on fire as they abandoned their former capital.

The Grey Eagles and other volunteer fire brigades were important for municipal safety, in at least one instance handling huge fires while Montgomery's white firefighters were in Mobile celebrating Mardi Gras. Respect and honor, ingrained in the unwritten baseball codes, were embraced by volunteer firemen, who formed ball teams to keep fit. The Grey Eagles regularly visited other cities to compete in firefighting events where baseball was soon a feature.

Playing games at family, church, and social gatherings, baseball clubs were embraced by communities. Teams became interwoven with society, and their games were exciting and entertaining for viewers. What began as curious sidelines to other events, such as picnics or fairs, were now the highlights. By the mid-1880s, fans of all races and genders were enjoying baseball as a spectator sport.

Across Alabama, Baseball Branches Out in the 1880s

Alabama baseball had sprouted roots and was branching out. The Huntsville club beat Nashville in August 1881 to earn a whopping $300 prize and gained a reputation as a "fast team." Jimmy Binford was their third baseman in 1883.

The Selma Dukes visited Huntsville in 1881. A round-trip train ticket was available for the many fans who wanted to see the game. In September, Huntsville returned the favor, visiting Selma, who won 46–7 in front of a large crowd at their Pastime Grounds.

The Eufaula Champions hosted Americus (Georgia) in 1882. Americus won 6–4, and the game took more than three hours. The following year, Union Springs opposed the Eufaula Champions at the Eufaula fairgrounds in order to accommodate the large crowd. Eufaula won that high-scoring affair 28–27.

Huntsville's Red Stockings hosted Chattanooga in 1883, and Memphis also visited Huntsville for games that year.

Selma's Stephens Base Ball Club made a trip to oppose Chattanooga in 1883.

The Union Springs team utilized the most modern equipment innovations when catcher James Holtzclaw wore a facemask while catching for pitcher Howard Shortridge in an 1883 game. The *Herald* of Union Springs raved about his ability to "almost pick the ball off of the bat" as he stands "right up under the batsman" and proclaimed him the best catcher in the state.

In 1884, the Eufaula Starlight club offered a challenge to face any team and then headed to Columbus, Georgia, to play for a prize of fifty dollars.

In north Alabama, Moulton hosted Landersville and was defeated in game two of an 1884 doubleheader that began with a match between the white teams from each city.

Huntsville catcher Charles Hutchins was with the J.W. McAllisters team in 1884 until he jumped to the Red Stockings in 1885. Hutchins's company later constructed a Black school in Huntsville.

In June 1885, Anniston sent its club to Jacksonville, Florida, losing 32–9.

In August 1885, the Eutaw Euphrates visited the Tuskegee Athletes, who beat them 19–6.

When Columbiana faced the Shelby Iron Works team in 1886, it was a sign that the gentleman's game had become fully embraced by the working class.

W.C. Alexander captained the 1889 Cannonball club in Jacksonville, Alabama.

Montgomery's First League Team, the Montgomery Blues

The *Montgomery Advertiser* mentioned Montgomery hosting the Memphis Eclipse in June 1886. The series opened the Southern League of Colored Base Ballists season, the very first multi-state African American baseball league in the nation. It would be six years before Montgomery would enter a white team into league play. Advertisements for the June 12 "Championship" game at Clisby Park mentioned the price of twenty-five

TEENAN JONES

Born into slavery in Tuscumbia, Alabama, in 1861, Henry Teenan Jones moved to Chicago after his emancipation and helped establish that city as a hub of Black entertainment, including baseball. As a player, Teenan Jones was a pitcher and outfielder with various Chicago-based teams. However, he would become much more notable for his many business ventures, including elevating the Chicago Unions to the heights of Black baseball as their president from 1884 to 1896.

Teenan Jones was a pioneer entrepreneur. His Elite Cafés were among the most (in)famous black-and-tan clubs in the country and perhaps the first cabarets to host jazz music. Jones had a newspaper column, wrote popular songs, funded early Black films, owned Chicago's Pekin Theater, and operated upscale Hyde Park restaurants and gambling houses, which catered to all races.

Jones was heavily involved in the numbers racket and an associate of Bronzeville numbers czar Mushmouth Johnson. He also rubbed shoulders with celebrities such as boxer Jack Johnson and musician Jelly Roll Morton, among others. In 1917, Jones was part of a vice sweep that exposed top politicians and police officials, forcing his retirement from business.

cents; ladies were admitted free. The race of the teams was not mentioned, as it was apparently expected to be understood. Montgomery's Clisby Park, near North Perry Street, hosted baseball for all races, as well as horse racing and other events such as fireworks shows and political speeches.

Reporters in Montgomery newsrooms were completely overwhelmed with incoming baseball news and began charging money to print game reports and team information. As a result, little is known about Montgomery's first league team beyond the results of the first series: one win, one loss, and one tie in a game shortened due to weather. The victory in game one was the first documented Montgomery win in any league game. No final score was noted, and no box scores are available.

Hale Infirmary in Montgomery, founded by Dr. Cornelius Dorsette, stood near Boguehome. *Alabama Department of Archives and History.*

Leading the Montgomery Blues club at this time was Dr. Cornelius Dorsette as team president, a physician and educator active in promoting literacy. Dr. Dorsette, known as the first licensed Black doctor in Montgomery, founded Hale Infirmary in 1890, one of the earliest facilities in the state to offer medical care to Black citizens. Team officials also included T. Stone as the field manager, as well as J. Addis Duncan, E.P. Morrison, and F.L. Lewis.

Improved roads and rail service across the South made travel possible but not lucrative, and teams in the fledgling league struggled financially. Ranging from South Carolina to Louisiana required too much travel, so teams dropped out as the circuit failed and disbanded in August. The league was reorganized in 1887, but little information was publicized. Following the loop's demise, the Montgomery Blues faced teams such as Atlanta and New Orleans as independents.

1888: MONTGOMERY BLUES MEET GEORGIA MINSTRELS

Montgomery played an exhibition game against the Georgia Minstrels theater troupe to promote the minstrels' evening show at the Opera House Theater. While many minstrel shows were overtly racist, the Georgia Minstrels styled their performances to subvert stereotypes and leave audiences questioning social norms and prejudices. The Georgia Minstrels were so popular that their name later became a catch-all phrase for any minstrel group with Black actors wearing blackface, setting them apart from previous mostly white performers. Minstrels playing baseball was a novel way to advertise a performance and also introduced the ballplayers to the power of including props, costumes, exaggerated motions, and witty banter for entertainment value.

Playing to attract crowds for their Montgomery theater performance, the Georgia Minstrels helped inspire theatrics in baseball. *University of Texas at Arlington Libraries, Special Collections.*

COLORED FEMALE BASEBALL CLUB

The *Montgomery Advertiser* mentioned a Fourth of July contest at Clisby Park between women's teams in 1889. The game, between teams chosen from members of the Colored Female Base Ball Club, was a featured event, although no game results were publicized. It's not the only report of Black women's baseball clubs in Alabama or even in Montgomery. Most women's clubs, however, preferred quiet fields with fewer fans to heckle or ogle.

1889: Local Rivalries

Wetumpka and Prattville met in July, resulting in a 36–16 drubbing of Wetumpka, according to the *Prattville Progress*. Another popular in-state rivalry between the cities of Troy and Union Springs was emerging. They played at a Union Springs picnic, where a big crowd watched Troy win 20–18. In Tuscaloosa, a game against nearby Blockton attracted a large crowd to the lakefront field. It was a lively, high-scoring affair, won by Tuscaloosa, 64–33, who scored a decisive forty runs in the first two innings.

CHAPTER 3

1890s

Unions Cement Steel City Reputation

The Birmingham Unions built a loyal following while facing teams from across the South, helping establish the city as a baseball force. In May 1897, the Birmingham Unions hosted Montgomery for a doubleheader, winning both games at West End Park in front of a large crowd. Following the victories, the *Birmingham News* declared the Unions "one of the strongest colored teams in the South now."

Birmingham's Unions visited Selma in May, accompanied by a large group of fans. Just a few weeks later, the Unions hosted the Pensacola Acmes in a series at West End Park.

The following season, 1898, the Birmingham Unions were facing Columbus (Mississippi) when things got out of hand. After plenty of miscues and errors by both sides, the Unions brawled on the field with their Columbus opponents following a close call. The fans also started a few "scraps" themselves, with fights in the bleachers and the grandstand. The final score of 7–6 left the Unions on the losing side.

In 1898, the Birmingham Unions also faced clubs from Nashville and Atlanta. Teams were willing to travel to oppose the Unions, who had a reputation for being a powerful foe as well as attracting lucrative crowds.

1890s Colored Base-Ball Club of Montgomery: The Blues Players

Billed as a crack team featuring the best pitcher in the South, Oscar "Hawk" Molette, along with star catcher Willie Patterson, the Montgomery Blues toured the region and entered league play years before many cities had teams. Playing in Montgomery, the Blues hosted the top clubs in the South, drawing large crowds. The Blues traveled to every neighboring state, offering many their very first look at Black baseball. In 1891, the Montgomery Blues visited Birmingham's Hornets, losing 11–10 in one of the earliest recorded contests between the two longtime rivals. The Blues, accompanied by a large excursion of Montgomery supporters, visited Pensacola that summer, falling 7–4 at Kupfrian's Park. In 1892, the Blues beat Goodloe's Birmingham Grays in Birmingham in front of more than five hundred fans, Montgomery's Hawk Molette and Birmingham's Robert Townsend were pitching.

The *Montgomery Advertiser* ran an announcement in 1893 that the reorganized Colored Base-Ball Club of Montgomery was issuing a traditional baseball challenge to any club in the South. It included a full list of its players and officers, possibly the earliest published roster of a Black baseball team in Alabama. Among them was J. Addis Duncan.

Addis Duncan's Razor

Montgomery game reports mention Addis Duncan as early as 1886. Duncan and William Patterson were the pitcher-catcher battery for a huge Blues game in Atlanta in '87. Duncan was the team leader, its captain, and its star player for ten years.

James Addis Duncan listed waiter and manual laborer as his formal occupations. He was popular around the city's night spots for his sporting nature, be it baseball, pool, dice, or poker. That nature would lead to danger often, as Addis Duncan found himself involved in several violent events, starting with a vicious barroom brawl in 1888.

The fight took place on a Saturday night in November at a local hangout called Johnson's Barrel House, downtown across from city hall on Monroe Street, known at the time as "Whisky Avenue" in the heart of Montgomery's Bowery area.

The location of the Addis Duncan bar brawl on Monroe Street in Montgomery, an area known as "Whisky Avenue" in the 1890s. *Author's photo, 2024.*

Duncan's teammate Willie Patterson was shooting pool when his opponent, George Williams, offered to put money on the game. Patterson said he doesn't have money and asked if anyone nearby would loan him fifty cents. A dollar was tossed from a nearby table, and a voice says, "Bet the whole dollar." Williams, leaning on his pool cue, loudly announced that he wasn't planning on playing against the entire crowd and included a few choice insults for the room.

Addis Duncan stood and addressed Williams, saying that there was no need for harsh words as no one in the bar had said anything offensive toward Williams, but he added, "If they did say anything, that's none of your [Williams's] business!" George Williams then approached Duncan shaking his fist, saying that he would "make it my business."

Duncan took a swipe at Williams and missed, maybe intentionally maybe not, followed by Williams landing a solid punch that staggered Addis Duncan, knocking him to the floor. Williams pounced quickly, beating Duncan furiously until the two men were separated.

Pushed out of the front door, George Williams waited just outside the bar. Soon Addis Duncan appeared, beaten and bruised from the previous pummeling. Williams, without a word, stepped in front of the door and put his hand in his hip pocket. Seeing that, Addis Duncan swiftly pulled a straight razor from his own back pocket and cut Williams's neck deeply, from the right ear to left side of the neck. A second flash of the razor sliced Williams's cheek under his left eye and down the jawbone. Duncan then applied his razor a third time, slashing across his victim's nose and under the right eye.

George Williams, described as a well-known bricklayer, was seemingly unfazed by Addis Duncan's razor or the streaming blood now drenching him with crimson. He grabbed Addis Duncan's shirt collar in one hand and beat Duncan repeatedly in the face with the other as he dragged Addis into the street.

A bystander attempted to end the brutal attack by striking Williams on the back of the skull with the butt of a pool cue. George Williams turned to take on the crowd, but loss of blood finally caused him to pass out in the street. The badly beaten Addis Duncan quickly made his exit before the police arrived.

Williams, at death's door for days, lost nearly a gallon of blood, and many expected a murder warrant to be imminent. However, George Williams refused to die and made a recovery at the hands of physician Dr. W.G. Bibb. The *Montgomery Advertiser* headlines led with "Addis Duncan's Razor," and many papers detailed the gruesome scene.

A warrant was issued for Addis Duncan, not for murder but for assault. Yet before the incident could come to trial, George Williams found trouble again, this time at Nickel's Hill near Lower Wetumpka Road. George Williams and Green McDonald were both seeing the same girl, although both were married men.

After a night of drinking, the two began to argue about the girl, and when the inevitable fight ensued, Williams, who was African American, announced that he "never proposed to let any damned negro carve him again" and drove his large pocketknife into Green McDonald's back. Then Williams slashed deeply into McDonald's throat and stabbed his cheek before dashing for the exit, leaving Green McDonald bleeding on the floor. Williams skipped town to avoid prosecution, and when he didn't reappear, Addis Duncan's case was dropped.

Five years later, the same year he was listed with the CBBCM team, Addis Duncan was once again wielding his razor. On Christmas Day 1893, Duncan's wife approached him with a letter she had received from a woman named Mary Graves. Graves ran a well-known brothel near the state capitol. Graves's letter was reportedly an offer from a white client who wanted to meet Addis Duncan's wife.

Addis Duncan went to Mary Graves's Pelham Street brothel, letter in hand. He found Graves easily and confronted her. The two argued, and Duncan pulled out his razor. By the time the authorities arrived, Mary Graves was badly cut. Addis Duncan willingly surrendered.

On January 13, 1894, the courtroom was filled with spectators as the judge discharged the case against Addis Duncan, holding that "there was an unwritten law as strong as the code, which gave to every man the right to tread upon the crawling viper of infamy and the power to stamp it as he would a real one," according to the *Montgomery Advertiser*. It was not Addis Duncan's last encounter with danger and the law.

In February 1897, Addis Duncan and his brother Eugene were back on Whisky Avenue in Montgomery's Bowery, playing poker at T.J. Kelly's saloon at 24 Monroe Street. Just before one o'clock in the morning, a shot rang out, followed by a barrage of nearly a dozen more gunshots in the bar. Reporters and police were on the scene in mere moments. They found Addis

Dixie Bar advertisement from 1890s, the location of Addis Duncan's barroom shootout in Montgomery's bowery. *Author's collection.*

View of the Monroe Street location of Addis Duncan's barroom shootout. *Author's photo, 2024.*

Duncan standing over the bullet-ridden body of Preston Jenkins, a smoking revolver in his hand.

Addis Duncan surrendered willingly, giving up his pistol, in which police discovered just two empty shells. Preston was shot five times, and Eugene Duncan fled amid the chaos following the gunfight and was assumed to have fired the other three shots. Eugene Duncan soon turned himself in.

The victim, Preston Jenkins, was also armed. Police found his pistol freshly emptied, with five bullet casings still hot to the touch. Jenkins, who owned a store on Decatur Street in Boguehome, survived long enough to give his account to the police, describing being shot at from both sides as Eugene stood behind him by the door of the bar, with Addis Duncan facing him on the other side of the room. Jenkins said that he emptied his pistol wildly after being hit by Eugene's gunshots from behind. One of Addis Duncan's two shots missed its target entirely and the other was a glancing wound, but when Jenkins died, both Duncan brothers were charged with murder.

Addis Duncan did not come to trial for the death of Preston Jenkins. Addis Duncan died while incarcerated, with no reason for his death announced. James Addis Duncan's funeral was held on February 25, 1898, at Old Ship Church, the oldest African American congregation in Montgomery, next door to the Duncan family home.

After waiting more than a year in jail, Eugene Duncan was finally brought to trial. Six weeks after Addis's funeral, on April 8, 1898, an all-white jury needed only ten minutes to find Eugene not guilty. Eugene Duncan went on to be a well-known and widely liked saloon keeper, running popular Montgomery taverns until his passing in 1918.

OTHER MONTGOMERY BLUES

Henry Troy, composer and baseball player. *International Center of Photography (NYC).*

Listed as Montgomery's second baseman, HENRY TROY would later gain fame as a composer, singer, and stage actor. Born in Montgomery in 1879, Troy worked as a lyricist with jazz legend Fletcher Henderson to co-write the song "Gin House Blues," which Henderson recorded with blues singer Bessie Smith in 1926. Troy went on to pen many songs and enjoyed success as a performer and composer until his passing in 1960.

Team officials included President J.W. JONES. Born into slavery in 1842 in North Carolina, Jones arrived in Alabama before the Civil War. Following his emancipation, Jones acquired a sizeable plantation in Haynesville, Alabama, where he opened a mercantile store, built and operated a track for horseracing, and became a medical doctor.

Jones was elected as state senator for Lowndes County in 1872 but also kept a family home at 341 South Jackson Street in Montgomery, near what would later be Dr. Martin Luther King Jr.'s Dexter Avenue parsonage. Dr. Jones was a prominent voice promoting voting rights, literacy, education, and women's health as both lecturer and educator. Respected in politics, Dr. Jones engaged the community through civic groups such as Knights of Pythias and encouraged public health with activities such as baseball.

Blues Vice-President FRANK LAKE was a Montgomery restaurateur and noted chef, opening a string of eateries that often bore his name. Chef Lake enjoyed continued success in Montgomery through the turn of the century; several locations that Chef Lake operated still serve today, although new

The Legacy Museum at the location where Chef Lake's restaurant formerly stood in Montgomery. *Author's photo, 2024.*

buildings now stand in their places. The Lake family home at 523 Pollard Street is now the popular Davis Café. In 1887, Frank and his wife, Annie, ran a restaurant at 431 North Court Street in Montgomery, a location now home to the Legacy Museum.

Willie Patterson, who was playing pool the night of Addis Duncan's first bar fight, was a well-known catcher. From the late 1880s through the mid-1890s, Patterson was a star among Alabama ballplayers, starting in the Montgomery Blues' biggest games. In August 1904, thirty-year-old William Patterson of 520 Holt Street in Montgomery shot and killed his wife, Minto, in an argument over fifty cents in the family kitchen. He rushed out the back door in his stocking feet, never to be seen again.

Oscar "Hawk" Molette (sometimes "Malett" or "Mollette") was the star pitcher for Montgomery and one of Alabama's top Black players of the era.

Born in about 1869, likely near Montgomery, Oscar got into trouble as a teen when he stabbed another boy and was arrested. The victim recovered, and it's unknown how the underage Molette was punished. By the time Oscar Molette reached eighteen, he was pitching for Montgomery's Blues. At the age of twenty-four, Molette was often described as the "most noted negro pitcher in the South," pitching some of the Montgomery Blues' biggest games, such as the Selma firemen's picnic.

Starring with the Montgomery Blues in games across the Southeast, Hawk Molette was instrumental in introducing Black baseball to white fans. In 1904, Oscar "Hawk" Molette caught a fever and did not recover, dying in Montgomery on September 22 at the age of thirty-two.

Lesser-Known Blues Players

Jonathan Meadows was possibly among those murdered in 1889 as part of a random violent crime spree by a man named Ben Elzy, who killed four in two states, resulting in Elzy's execution.

Also listed with the Montgomery club were James Hannon and Watt Buchanan, who appeared in a later reorganization of the club.

George Kelly played with Montgomery as an infielder; later he was a popular local musician, playing piano in venues around the city.

Henry Allen, later a well-known Montgomery bartender, played third base and catcher and served as team captain.

John C. Alexander was an infielder and served as team treasurer.

The Prince Robinson on the team wasn't the actual Prince Robinson; someone concealed his identity by borrowing the name of the well-known Birmingham resident and future "Singing Barber" of the U.S. Capitol.

Montgomery Reorganizes

In 1897, the club reported its organizational meetings to the press. Offering a rare view into the roster progression of a nineteenth-century Black baseball team, the article mentioned familiar names as well as new ones.

The Montgomery club had John Alexander at first base, Will Meadows at second, Willie Watkins as shortstop, and Henry Allen at third. The outfield consisted of Willie Hall in center, Russell Buchanan in left, and James Hannon in right. Willie Johnson was catcher, with Watt Buchanan, Dave Lowe, and Robert Campbell as pitchers. Jim Patton was listed as utility man.

Several players remained from the previous announcement: pitcher Watt Buchanan, first baseman John Alexander, and third baseman Henry Allen. Willie Hall was still team captain, a full five years later. Hall was a popular player, also appearing with Chicago, New Orleans, and other clubs. Among the newcomers was Jim Patton, who later played with the

An 1897 baseball equipment advertisement in Montgomery. *Author's collection.*

Philadelphia Giants and Birmingham Unions. Also on the team was right fielder James Hannon.

Team officers included N.E. Abercrombie as president. Nicholas Abercrombie worked as secretary of the Alabama Literary Society of Montgomery and was a post office clerk.

1890s Across Alabama

Baseball thrived across Alabama in the 1890s, with multiple teams in nearly every city and town. The games became immensely popular, and reports flowed from all corners.

However, some clubs were still developing, leaving fans and reporters perplexed when teams opposed less talented aggregations. When team captain Willie Coleman took his 1890 Uniontown club on the road and defeated the Marion team in a lopsided 45–5 tilt, the *Canebrake Herald* gleefully declared Uniontown "champion colored nine of the blackbelt" area. Conversely, when Piedmont defeated the Spring Garden club that summer, Piedmont newspapers accused Spring

Garden of playing "a very poor game" in the 59–11 contest that had to be ended after seven innings due to darkness.

In 1891, Spring Garden was defeated on an Independence Day visit to nearby Piedmont, "clad in uniforms that were poems in color," according to the *Piedmont Inquirer*. Piedmont also played a home-away series with Anniston that summer.

The 1892 town fair in Bessemer offered a twenty-five-dollar purse for the winning team in a game held at Twenty-Fifth Street and Eleventh Avenue.

Rivalries were fierce, evidenced by an 1892 contest between Greenville and Evergreen clubs. When the Friday morning game at Greenville was about to get underway, a full-fledged brawl broke out between the teams. During the melee, Adams of Greenville produced a knife and badly slashed Evergreen's Ellis, requiring a doctor. Other players fought each other with bats, knocking several men to the ground. Police arrived, removed the crowd from the field, and arrested the players. Both teams made bond by lunchtime and returned to the field to play the game in the afternoon.

Evergreen visited Brewton in 1892 for a September game to close the season. The round-trip cost eighty-five cents, and a large crowd was expected to travel with the team.

Selma's club, managed by Bud Huffman in 1893, had King Callen (called "the king of first basemen") ahead of their game against Montgomery. Selma pitcher A.J. Howard got the starting assignment. Admission was twenty-five cents.

The Ozark Rabbits beat the Dothan Lamplighters by two runs, according to reports in the *Ozark Banner-Register* in May 1894. Dothan was also beaten by the Columbia (Alabama) club that summer.

Greensboro's Charter Oaks hosted games at the city's train depot, defeating Uniontown in 1894. Greensboro traveled to Tuscaloosa for a doubleheader the following year. Benjamin Barnes was the shortstop for Tuscaloosa's Blues in 1894 and Elvira Brown their top pitcher.

In 1895, Gadsden and Jacksonville (Alabama) faced off for an Independence Day contest that was largely attended. Gadsden won easily, scoring twenty-nine times against Jacksonville, who were only able to push a dozen runs across the plate.

Also in 1895, there was a hotly contested July game between Tuskegee and Union Springs. In the fifth inning, angry Tuskegee players left the field, refusing to continue. The umpire declared a forfeit in favor of the host, Union Springs, who had been leading the game behind their star pitcher, George Shorter Jr., before the dispute.

In one report from August 1895, the Montgomery Cracker Jacks defeated the Pensacola Acmes, 14–13. It was the only mention of Montgomery's Cracker Jacks.

More popular were the Montgomery Reds as organized by John H. Wilson and Frank S. Robinson. According to reports, the Reds were eagerly supported in the city. When they hosted the Memphis Cliffords in 1896, the Reds thanked Montgomery-area businesses for providing new uniforms.

In June 1896, Selma hosted Montgomery and then traveled to Atlanta and Birmingham for contests. The team was popular; it was noted that both Selma's St. James and Albert Hotels were so busy during game days that some arriving in the city had to find private rooms.

In Cherokee County in northeastern Alabama, the town of Centre and Howell's Crossroads community "crossed billets" in 1896, according to the *Coosa River News*. Centre won 15–13 behind the pitching of Porter McConnel and his "miasmatic curve."

In 1897, while some Montgomery Blues players had rebranded themselves as the Reds, the "colored" Montgomery Greys were also active in town, and the two teams faced off at least once during the summer.

Standing almost seven feet tall, Birmingham's Madison Sharp received ten months of hard labor in 1897 for breaking his bat over the head of an umpire following a call that went against him, according to the *Birmingham Post-Herald*.

The year 1898 saw Talladega's Haymakers accepting a challenge from Knoxville, defeating them in two games under manager John Boxley; Moses Kidd was the Haymakers' captain.

The 1898 Fairview team's Sam Young, a miner and railroad fireman, was one of the few nonwhites on a white team in Alabama. Born in 1873, Young was listed as "mulatto" on census reports, the only available choice besides "white" and "Negro."

Sam Young, standing back right with the white Fairview Alabama team in 1898, was noted as Black on his 1917 draft card. *Gadsden Public Library Archives Collection.*

In 1898, there were multiple reports about a brawl between teams in Wilcox County resulting in fifteen men shot, two fatally.

It wasn't just teams being rowdy. Sometimes crowds were just as rough. During an 1899 Birmingham game, two friends who were brothers-in-law became embroiled in an argument about the teams they were watching. When one man shot his friend in the leg, he instantly felt remorse and helped pick his victim up. However, nearby fans were concerned that there was a murder taking place. Realizing that his situation looked bad, the shooter took flight. The crowd was well prepared to defend itself, as more than one hundred firearms, including two Winchester rifles, were brought to bear at the fleeing shooter, who somehow managed to dodge and weave his way through the hail of bullets without being struck in order to make his escape. The wounded man recovered; his brother-in-law had much explaining to do but appears to have been let off for the crime.

In 1899, the Montgomery Greys faced a team from Tuskegee's Normal School at the Montgomery Normal School (later Alabama State University) athletic field.

Eufaula's Popular Team

The city of Eufaula's club hosted games at their field on "the bluff" overlooking the river that marks Alabama's border with Georgia. Eufaula's team also traveled, opposing Montgomery in 1898, with a large contingent of fans making the trip via train.

In 1899, Eufaula beat two teams in a single day. During the city's summer fair, Eufaula first downed Union Springs, 7–6, and then knocked off Ozark in a 25–15 slugfest. Several Eufaula players also participated in events such as sack races, greased pole climb, and the 250-yard dash. The popular Dick Bailey was Eufaula's star centerfielder.

Also in 1899, a Montgomery team was involved when two men died and six were sickened during a postgame dance in Eufaula. Following the party, eight men fell ill. It was learned that they had drunk medicinally laced wine, a gout remedy stolen from a druggist by a local, who was also sickened.

The victims included the two deceased, Claud Raines and Johnnie Fryer, as well as those sickened, Leroy Winn, John Grimes, Henry Thomas, William Crossley, and Dennis Wilson. It was a tragic story that overshadowed baseball's success at the close of the century.

Well, anyway, our colored ball club won a game.

The *Eufaula Daily Times* had a long history of questionable reporting, typified with its handling of a fatal postgame party.

The first thirty years of Black baseball in Alabama included steady rosters of well-organized teams, formal league efforts, and the building of social connections across the region and beyond. These important ingredients would be strengthened as the amateur game turned pro.

Boguehome

Two rookie Montgomery cops on foot patrol came across a dead cow.

"Send headquarters a message that we need a wagon," said one cop to the other.

"How do I spell where we are?"

After a pause, "I don't know. Let's drag this over to Hull Street. I can spell *that*!"

Also known as Bogahome, Boguehoma, Bugahoma, or Boga-homa, this section of Montgomery that was long ago one of the most notorious parts of town is now nearly forgotten. During the second half of the 1800s, repeated bouts of yellow fever often reached epidemic proportions. Public health efforts spurred land development and the popularity of exercise; a byproduct was the evolution of the neighborhood that would be home to Montgomery's Black baseball teams and help birth Alabama jazz music.

Seeking fresh air, affluent citizens developed neighborhoods on the hills surrounding downtown Montgomery. Increasing efforts to avoid infection found houses being built in large numbers. With names that reflected their lofty locations, Capitol Heights, Cottage Hill, Centennial Hill, and others were popular among middle- and higher-income families.

Nineteenth-century public transportation encouraged rapid expansion, resulting in wide spreads of unused low areas between the popular neighborhoods being erected on the hills overlooking downtown Montgomery. In between those hilltop neighborhoods with even rows of new houses, buildings in low-lying areas were abandoned by those who could afford to leave. What remained were dilapidated dwellings, usually near a well, creek, or one of Montgomery's many natural artesian springs. These old houses offered low- or zero-cost quarters for any who needed them.

One of those neighborhoods was the village of Boguehome. Adulterated from the French language or possibly Choctaw, or maybe taken from a French map of Choctaw land, the area known as Boguehome was situated six blocks south of the state capitol in an open, low-lying space with a nearby creek. This sparsely wooded plot was wild and open. Trees dotted Norman Bridge Road, mostly Osage orange, sugarberry, and hickory. The area was green and lush, a nearby creek rarely went dry and though unfit for humans offered year-round watering for wildlife and livestock, which roamed freely.

The creek has run there for centuries, becoming known as Genetta Creek after a lady named Ghenetta drowned in the mid-1800s. Repeated drownings forced the city to cover and line the brook with concrete to protect passersby as well as try to contain the constant flow of water.

The buildings were antiquated in design, ranging from makeshift wooden shanties to frontier log cabins and shotgun-style houses. Some faced the dirt road but most don't. Occasionally construction added a fresh neighbor among the dilapidated, creating a patchwork of old and new.

At the southern end of Boguehome, South Decatur and South Union Streets meet Norman's Bridge Road and Carter Hill Road, the main access

"Street in Boguehome," by Anne Goldthwaite, circa 1920. *Courtesy of the Montgomery Museum of Fine Arts.*

point to Montgomery from the south. A concrete post announcing "One Mile to Montgomery" stood nearby, making it a reasonable commute for those employed downtown. Often called the "Broadway of Boguehome" for its busy, eclectic scenes, South Union Street was a popular route to bring crops and livestock to market. Through the 1920s, large herds of cattle and other livestock were driven up the dusty road past the state capitol to be loaded onto trains or taken to one of north Montgomery's slaughterhouses. A blacksmith opened the first shop in Boguehome before 1880, and saloons soon began to appear, offering farmhands the first chance to spend their weekly pay. Gin houses milled vast amounts of cotton but frequently caught fire, with one spark creating infernos that burned to the ground in minutes, reducing the building and its contents to ashes amid the cheers of drunken onlookers.

On the rise just to the east of Boguehome was the State Normal School/Teachers College, now Alabama State University. Students used the vacant block bordering Boguehome for activities, including baseball. By the end of the century, the school Athletic Park occupied the lot, abutting Boguehome on Union Street.

Setting on the hill to the northeast of the wooded glen, close to the new houses in Montgomery's Centennial Hill neighborhood, was Hale Infirmary. It was one of the few medical facilities available to African Americans in Montgomery, its location now denoted with a historic marker.

The village of Boguehome housed a wide array of people. It was home to longtime residents with local connections dating to the early 1800s. Some Boguehome dwellers were white southerners who didn't care for authoritarian big-city rules. Still others were laborers working on farms nearby. Many residents were destitute, and this diverse hamlet became an attractive destination for itinerant hobos, vagrants, and outright criminals in search of refuge without questions.

A large portion were African Americans or forced-immigrant Africans with simply nowhere else to go. There was the gentleman who lost his feet to frostbite and was forced to rely on others, the kind old woman who daily made pork-belly sandwiches to give out to hungry passersby, one lady many suspected was a witch, and another who claimed to be a voodoo priestess.

Situated outside the city limits, beyond the reach of Montgomery sheriffs, Boguehome swiftly became a loose, multicultural outpost trading in farm equipment and booze, while also offering choices varying from prostitution to surgery and higher education. Juke joints settled in alongside livery stables and shotgun shacks, soon outnumbering them. Flophouses and brothels were available by the dozens, but there were just two tiny churches. Side streets with names like "Rat Alley" twisted through the growing maze of randomly placed buildings.

Gambling houses were easily found in what had become Montgomery's red-light district, and one of the most popular was "Noah's Ark," offering sleeping rooms upstairs with drinking below. Men wore pistols openly and often found excuses to use them. It was not unusual to see a horse being ridden into one of the many bars and whiskey joints. Bonfires were common at all times of year, lighting up the sky visible to most of Montgomery, whose citizens also heard the revelry of Boguehome, where in the 1920s a new American art form began emerging.

The song "Bugahoma Blues," recorded by the Black Birds of Paradise in July 1927, was inspired by the music heard in the juke joints of Boguehome, where the band often played. This song, along with four other Black Birds tracks, is among Alabama's first jazz recordings. Written by William "Buddy" Howard, the lively tune offers the listener a chance to enjoy of the vibrant

View of ASU baseball stadium overlooking Boguehome, circa 1960. *Alabama State University.*

scene of the Jazz Era in Montgomery as though they are walking past a row of Decatur Street juke joints in the 1920s.

The Black Birds of Paradise were an eight-piece Montgomery-based band of Tuskegee graduates led by "Buddy" Howard on trombone. Other members included James Bell and William Boyd on saxophones, Melvin Small on piano, Tom Ivery on banjo, Ivory Johnson on tuba, and drummer Sam Bordees. "Bugahoma Blues" features coronet player Philmore "Shorty" Hall, who would go on to teach trumpet to a high schooler named Dizzy Gillespie and later instructed jazz drumming legend Grady Tate. The band recorded the songs in a Birmingham hotel. "Bugahoma Blues" was released along with "Tishomingo Blues" in 1927. Their records, quite popular during their career, are now rare and highly sought by collectors.

Boguehome remained largely unchanged into the 1930s, a throwback village that streetcar planners avoided when laying tracks to affluent neighborhoods. South Union Street in Boguehome wasn't paved until 1936, when the area was cleared for Paterson Court housing, built by the PWA. The construction of Interstate 85 was controversially directed through Black neighborhoods in the 1960s, effectively obscuring the last remains of the old village of Boguehome.

CHAPTER 4

1900s

Montgomery's Blues and Birmingham's Giants Set the Stage

At the start of the twentieth century, baseball was an attraction. People came to watch big games in large numbers, creating revenue opportunities. For teams everywhere, profitability was an important factor. Funding trips to other cities while covering opponents' guarantees and other expenses involved in running a club was difficult, and now players demanded pay. Baseball had become a business; Alabama's teams and players would need to adapt in order to survive.

In May 1900, the *Birmingham News* reported that "the biggest excursion of the season" was due from Tennessee for the ballgame between Chattanooga and Birmingham. Fourteen passenger train cars were filled with people from Knoxville and Chattanooga going to the game.

Games were so popular that teams were sometimes forced to share fields, such as when the *Birmingham News* reported that a 1901 Birmingham Unions game was scheduled early so an Elks Club ballgame between the Fats and Leans could take place afterward.

Teams relied on facing popular foes to generate income. League clubs were encouraged to book games with non-league opponents; it was common practice even for major-league teams to host midseason exhibitions outside of league play. White-owned ballparks were an option, available at a fee and usually demanding a percentage of the gate receipts, but only when

View of Montgomery, Alabama, circa 1910. *Author's collection.*

the facilities weren't otherwise in use. Those parks could be hired for games expected to draw large crowds, offsetting the expense. Otherwise, teams had to search for available ballfields or build their own, both expensive propositions. Even after securing a field, other issues often popped up, requiring enterprising solutions.

In 1900, Montgomery's Street Railway was required to adhere to new segregation ordinances. Foreshadowing the Montgomery Bus Boycott, Black fans turned out to watch a free ballgame but avoided using the streetcars, arriving at the ballpark in large numbers of wagons and carriages. The Montgomery Street Railway Company, which also owned the ballpark, refused to allow the game to proceed. The company expected round-trip streetcar fares and denied any compromises. Fans offered to pay admission for the game that was announced as free, but the company spitefully canceled the game.

Big crowds and scheduling issues were motivators. In Montgomery, among the improvements was a major expansion of the Athletic Park at Montgomery's Normal School and soon a new West End Park. It wasn't just big cities where Black teams were finding ways to control their own businesses. In 1903, the *Alabama Beacon* reported that Lucius Jones fenced off an area south of the Greensboro train depot for use as the team's ballpark and praised the entrepreneur's effort.

Decades before walk-up music and jumbotrons, Wyer's Creole Cornet Band provided music for fans as Black entrepreneurs revolutionized the fan experience. *State Archives of Florida, Florida Memory.*

These venues, and others like them, gave teams a place to call home. Perhaps just as importantly, teams no longer had to share gate receipts, surrender premium dates, or kowtow to Jim Crow demands just to play baseball. They were a luxury many clubs were willing to travel for.

Also in 1900, Montgomery was defeated by visiting Pensacola in front of a large crowd, which didn't mind the final score because the legendary Pensacola Creole Band was on hand providing music during the game. Wyers Creole Coronet Band, organized in 1873, would tour for fifty years. It was a popular event; the band would often travel with the Pensacola team for Montgomery games.

Southern Colored Baseball League

The Colored Southern League was formed in the late 1890s and expanded across the South. By 1901, the circuit was ranging east as far as Charleston,

South Carolina, encompassing more than a dozen cities. League standings, player statistics, and game reports were sparse, as most teams had little to do with the league office. Things changed somewhat in 1905 as efforts were made to revive the Southern Colored Baseball League. The SCBL's large footprint across the south added Birmingham, Montgomery, and Mobile.

The league named Will Morton from New Orleans as president; among the league officers, Montgomery's E.J. Lewis was elected treasurer. Lewis was active in the leadership of the Knights of Pythias and held a trusted postal job. Lewis had also been principal of Montgomery's Madison Street School, teaching Black children since the late 1880s.

Birmingham's Unions were said to represent their city in the SCBL. The Unions fielded strong teams, often drawing large crowds of more than eight hundred fans to West End Park. However, the representative for Birmingham at the 1905 SCBL meetings listed as "Charles J. Taylor" is likely a misprint. Charles Isham "C.I." Taylor arrived in Birmingham the previous year and was one of the few men capable of handling the complex task of successfully organizing the perennially dysfunctional loop. Taylor's Birmingham Giants replaced the Birmingham Unions in the newly reorganized league, just as the Giants had usurped the Unions in popularity at their shared home field, the West End Park Slag Pile.

Montgomery's entry, the Blues, sometimes called the Hornets, became very popular and were invited to play at the spacious park on Madison Avenue (when the white ball team was on the road). In one notable game there, Montgomery's pitcher Lamar struck out fourteen Nashville Giants.

In July 1905, when Montgomery defeated Nashville, 2–0, at Washington Park, players named Hannon and Cobb were the top Montgomery performers. This was either outfielder James Hannon or young shortstop Henry Hannon Jr.; the Hannon name would continue to figure prominently in Montgomery's baseball scene over the next three decades. The "Cobb" is likely Lorenza S.N. "Willie" Cobb, who played and managed for many teams in his long career. With Montgomery, Cobb was a teenage infielder, but he was later an important team executive as well as a valuable member of the Negro Southern and Negro National Leagues' front offices. A Mississippi native, Cobb served in World War I with the all–African American 804th Pioneer Infantry.

Mobile's club suffered from a lack of press coverage. The team was represented at meetings by Edmund Turner, president of the Mobile Draymens union. The Mobile club was also dubbed the Hornets by the

WILLIAM CLARENCE MATTHEWS

Selma's William Clarence Matthews, seen with the 1903 Harvard team, is known as the "Jackie Robinson of his era." *Courtesy of the Harvard University Archives.*

Born in Selma in 1877, Matthews was a trailblazer in baseball and leader in American politics and law. Following the death of his father, William was educated at Tuskegee by Booker T. Washington before being admitted to Harvard University. At Harvard, William Matthews was among the first African Americans on the baseball and football teams. Matthews excelled on the diamond, leading the baseball team in batting average for three seasons while playing alongside future major leaguers. William Matthews scored the winning run against Yale in a game at New York's Polo Grounds, attended by more than nine thousand people. Matthews was considered the top prospect on the team, and the ***Boston Post*** called him "the greatest colored athlete of all time."

Matthews began playing professionally with the Burlington, Vermont team in 1905, the only Black player in the Northern League. On July 4, Matthews had three hits in his first game and continued his success throughout the summer. His prodigious hitting and slick fielding earned much praise, and soon the Boston Braves were rumored to be considering signing him.

Matthews was fully aware of how close he came to the major leagues. Amid rumors of being passed over by Boston due to his race, Matthews said, "I think it is an outrage that colored men are discriminated against in the big leagues. What a shame it is that black men are barred forever from participating in the national game."

Matthews worked his way through school, refusing offers that might invalidate his collegiate status. Matthews graduated from

William Clarence Matthews with the 1902 Harvard baseball team. *Courtesy of the Harvard University Archives.*

Harvard, attended Boston University School of Law, passed the bar exam in 1908, acted as legal counsel for Marcus Garvey's UNIA, and later became an assistant attorney general in Washington, D.C.

After William Matthews died suddenly in 1928, he was hailed as one of the leading Black voices in America. The Ivy League baseball championship trophy is now named in honor of William Clarence Matthews. Historians consider Matthews the "Jackie Robinson of his era" for his bright, but brief, baseball career.

Pensacola News ahead of the 1905 season opener between Mobile and the Pensacola team at Kupfrian's Park in Pensacola.

The league came to an abrupt end in August when an epidemic of yellow fever in New Orleans restricted travel in the South due to quarantine requirements.

1900–1909 Baseball Across Alabama Brings Big Crowds

Uniontown celebrated Independence Day 1900 by hosting a game against Selma, and the home team came away victorious. Stores closed early, and the game was one of the few events in the city, leading to a large crowd.

LaFayette's team visited Roanoke in 1902. The game was attended by a large number of fans, including many white spectators. Roanoke won 12–9, according to the *Roanoke Leader*. Two years later, the same teams were facing off when the Roanoke pitcher, an unnamed railroad camp worker, suffered a broken arm while delivering a pitch.

Pickensville borders Mississippi in western Alabama. Its popular team, led by John Herndon in 1903, reportedly vanquished several tough local opponents.

In April 1904, Bessemer hosted Chattanooga for a series at Lynch's Park. Many fans were on hand to watch the contests and were entertained by a brass band that traveled with Chattanooga.

Fort Payne was defeated 6–4 at home by nearby Battelle (Alabama) in June 1905, according to the *Ft. Payne Journal*.

Among the earliest images of Black baseball in Alabama is the Hobson Park game postcard circa 1909. Incorporated in 1899, Hobson City was Alabama's first Black-governed town. *Author's collection.*

The Tuskegee University team in 1908 was one of many talented teams in Alabama. *Author's collection.*

The New York Americans, later known as the New York Yankees, were training in Montgomery in 1905 when Clark Griffith and members of his team stopped at Highland Oval to watch a game between Black teams.

While the game had developed into a business, southern cordiality never went out of style. A 1905 article covering the L&N Railroad picnic in Greenville reported that the Montgomery team was defeated by the Greenville Hornets in a close game. The newspaper, the *Greenville Advocate*, noted that one of the Montgomery railroad men "requested us to say that they had an exceedingly good time, and the best of order was maintained."

Birmingham was the scene for a big game between the Anniston Giants and Atlanta in 1906. The two clubs faced off at West End Park, with Atlanta the victor, 5–2. Anniston's Giants also had Birmingham-based series against Tuscaloosa's Giants, Macon (Georgia), and the St. Louis Giants that summer.

In southern Alabama, teams from Elba and Enterprise were reported in a 1906 game, with Elba winning at home, 17–11.

Anniston and Macon (Georgia) chose a neutral site, West End Park in Birmingham, for their June 1906 series, after defeating the St. Louis Giants there in May.

There was no denying Black baseball's popularity in Birmingham after 1,400 fans showed up for a game between the Birmingham Giants and Atlanta Baptist College (now Morehouse University) in 1908. According to the *Birmingham Post Herald*, Birmingham won the game 4–1 behind "Steel Arm" Johnny Taylor and the Taylor brothers. The next day, the Giants again downed the collegiates, 5–1.

CHAPTER 5

GIANTS AND STARS

A Meeting of Giants

It was an important event when the Leland Giants of Chicago faced the Birmingham Giants in 1909. Future Hall of Famer Rube Foster pitched for Leland, facing "Cyclone" Williams of Birmingham at West End Park. The Lelands beat Birmingham with scores of 3–0 and 4–2 in front of large crowds. Later in the year, Birmingham faced the Lelands in Indianapolis for five games, earning a level of revenge by winning three from Rube Foster's squad. More important than the games was the connection that would propel all of Black baseball to its next level.

The Birmingham Giants, under C.I. Taylor and his brothers, were instrumental in advancing baseball's popularity in Birmingham. Taylor was a pioneer of scouting and coaching. Chicago's Rube Foster was one of the top baseball stars in the country, and his Leland Giants were among the strongest teams in all of baseball. Taylor and Foster, equally respected as ability assessment geniuses, both stocked their teams with highly talented players. This meeting between these two brilliant baseball men was an important development for the sport.

1910: Montgomery Stars Have Taylor Connection

The Montgomery Stars appear in the *Montgomery Times* with a 1910 announcement. Articles mention games against clubs such as Brewton, Troy, and Selma. The Stars lineup included John Cunningham at second base, Taylor at third base, Nickens in left field, Hartford in right, Manuel in centerfield, Cox at shortstop, and Staples at first base. Marion Cunningham and Kelly are catchers, and pitchers listed are Jones, Battle, and Collins, who also played as catcher. The early appearance of the Cunninghams is notable, as they will be fixtures in Montgomery box scores for years to come. First baseman Staples is John Staples, who later is connected with running the team.

Curious is the player named Taylor at third base for Montgomery, the last name of four legendary brothers closely connected to Alabama baseball and pillars of the Negro Leagues, one of whom is a Hall of Famer.

"Taylor third base" is possibly twenty-six-year-old "Candy Jim" Taylor, for whom we have incomplete info for that season and who was known as a third baseman. It's also possibly his brother, then twenty-one, future Hall of Famer Ben Taylor, who also has only a few documented games that year. Both Jim and Ben Taylor are lacking in credited games that season, making identification difficult. South Carolina's Taylor brothers are baseball royalty, known as the "first family of Negro League baseball." They played with, against, or managed the biggest names in the sport. It's uncertain which of the Taylor brothers may have played for Montgomery, but all are crucial to baseball in Alabama.

The eldest, Charles Isham "C.I." Taylor, was a pioneer in scouting college athletes. An educated and polished gentleman who served honorably as a Buffalo Soldier during the Spanish-American War and was a thirty-third-degree Mason, "C.I." Taylor was instrumental in organizing the Colored Southern League, Negro National League, and Negro Southern League. He founded the Birmingham Giants in 1904 and ushered Birmingham into baseball's limelight with his brilliant managing and scouting acumen.

The next eldest, John "Steel Arm Johnnie" Taylor, pitched professionally until age forty-five and managed many excellent teams. John Taylor took part in some of the most iconic events in baseball history. With Birmingham's Giants, "Steel Arm" Taylor was the ace of the pitching staff and one of the best moundsmen in baseball.

The second youngest, "Candy Jim" Taylor, had a stellar forty-year career. He played and/or managed in nearly two thousand games. Jim's twenty-

The four Taylor brothers founded the Birmingham Giants and remained closely connected to Alabama. *From left to right*: "Candy" Jim, "Steel Arm" John, Charles Isham "C.I.," and Ben Taylor. *From the Indianapolis Freeman, 1910.*

seven seasons as a manager are the most by any African American in any baseball league. Simply a legend in baseball, Candy Jim Taylor was one of the greatest managers in history.

The youngest was slugging first baseman/pitcher Ben Taylor, whose twenty-one-year playing career was so outstanding that in 2006 he was enshrined in Major League Baseball's Hall of Fame. Ben Taylor hit .300 or better in sixteen seasons, amassed more than 1,200 hits, and was an exceptionally smooth fielder.

Montgomery Levels Up

In 1910, the Montgomery Stars (sometimes listed as the Hornets) hosted Rube Foster's Leland Giants, losing 7–3 at the hands of the Giants star, legendary African American athlete Robert "Bobby" Marshall. Marshall later played in the very first National Football League game (1920) to become the first Black player in the NFL. Bobby Marshall also played professional baseball with St. Paul's Colored Gophers alongside Candy Jim Taylor.

SPRUDELS AND PLUTOS SPARK ALABAMA'S BEST BALL TEAMS

C.I. Taylor and his brothers relocated in 1910, moving the Birmingham Giants to Indiana to become the West Baden Sprudels, sponsored by a resort spa that sold bottled spring water called "Sprudel Water." Their rival, a resort in nearby French Lick that marketed "Pluto Water" tonic, called their team the French Lick Plutos.

Employed as hotel staff and playing ballgames to entertain elite guests and high-rolling gamblers, the West Baden Sprudels and French Lick Plutos included many future Alabama stalwarts such as Dizzy Dismukes, Joe Scotland, Henry Hannon Jr., Lorenza Cobb, John Cunningham, and James Patton. The French Lick Sprudels took on younger players such as Marion Cunningham, Bunny Downs, Stringbean Williams, and Johnny Goodgame, all of whom would later wear Montgomery and/or Birmingham uniforms. Manager "C.I."

After the Birmingham Giants became the West Baden Sprudels, they featured many Alabama players. *From left to right*: C.I. Taylor, Dizzy Dismukes, unidentified, Will McMurray, Morten Clark, Jim Taylor, unidentified (possibly Lorenza Cobb), Ben Taylor, Marion Cunningham, Bennie Lyons, and Andrew "String Bean" Williams. *Author's collection.*

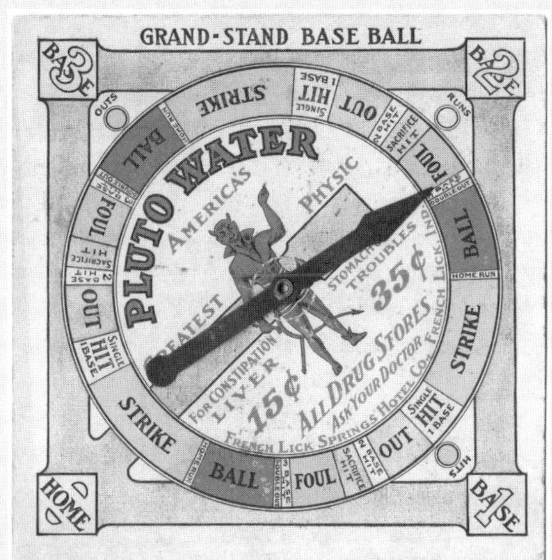

French Lick Plutos baseball game toy spinner. *Library Company of Philadelphia.*

Taylor's Sprudels got a top-level baseball education, as five future Hall of Famers graced the Sprudels roster under Taylor.

The Sprudels and Plutos featured some of baseball's greatest players and faced top clubs, even defeating white major-league teams at luxurious resort ballparks. The Plutos and Sprudels were high-stakes training grounds for Alabama's most legendary Negro League teams and players who would reshape the game.

In 1910, the Montgomery Stars club hosted an unusual opponent: the St. Louis Black Bloomer Girls. Women's teams, whose players wore skirts with bloomers underneath, were a popular draw for exhibition games. The St. Louis Black Bloomer Girls who took the field in Montgomery against the Stars were the St. Louis Black Broncho club, a respected ball team of (mostly) women who toured the country.

In February 1911, the *Freeman News* of Indianapolis ran a small ad with contact information for Montgomery Stars manager W. Cobb at an address near the Normal School Athletic Park. Lorenza "Willie" Cobb, newly appointed manager of the Montgomery Stars, was seeking teams to schedule games with the advert. The ad appeared to pay off when the Stars organized a string of exhibition series. Traveling to St. Louis, the Montgomery Stars squared off against one of the top lineups in baseball and were soundly defeated in both games.

Rube Foster was the top pitching star in Black baseball, leading the 1910 Chicago Leland Giants on national tours. *Twin City Star staff photographer, public domain, via Wikimedia Commons.*

In the opposing dugout, there were some familiar faces. Among the St. Louis Stars were two of the famous Taylor brothers, "Candy" Jim and "Steel Arm" Johnny. Perhaps the ad wasn't important after all, the Taylors and Montgomery's Willie Cobb having just been teammates in West Baden. These connections served them all well. Cobb, Hannon, and the Taylors would continue to share scouting information and schedule games together for many years.

The Montgomery Stars hosted another high-profile opponent, the Brooklyn Royal Giants, billed as the reigning "colored champions of the East." The Stars faced the Royal Giants for two April games in 1911. Brooklyn's Royal Giants, a popular barnstorming team, were among the best in the nation.

The Brooklyn business secretary was Nat Strong, a white man who would later take control of the Royal Giants and became one of the most prolific (and notorious) owner/promoters in Negro League baseball. For years, Nat Strong was the only contact teams could use to book games in New York, holding a virtual monopoly for games in that area. It was an arrangement that did not escape criticism, especially with Strong charging a hefty percentage for approving the contests and nixing games that might overshadow his Royal Giants. It is unknown what experience Nat Strong had with the Montgomery club; however, this is one of the era's rare instances involving Montgomery facing a New York team until after Strong's 1935 demise.

CHAPTER 6

1915

Grey Sox Snare Pennant to Weave New Dynasty

When the Montgomery Grey Sox first appeared in local newspapers in 1915, it was the start of a long and successful run. Organized by Montgomery's Henry Hannon, the club faced a YMCA team in a July game featuring the Cunningham brothers appearing together for the first time. Facing the Grey Sox, YMCA pitcher Horace "Underhand Sail Ball Demon" May outdueled "The Great" Cotton.

The Montgomery Grey Sox lost that game but won others often, and more people started attending games. A large crowd was on hand for the September 14 no-hitter thrown by Grey Sox pitcher Cotton against the Mobile All-Stars. "The Great" Cotton won 3–0 while walking just one Mobile hitter, authoring the first documented no-hit game by an African American pitcher in Montgomery's history.

David "The Great" Cotton pitched for Montgomery and later umpired Negro League games. *Courtesy of W.J. Plott.*

The Grey Sox star hurler "The Great" Cotton, also known as David Cotton, was supported in the rotation by pitchers John Goodgame and lefty James Patton. Patton was the starting centerfielder but was known for throwing a good spitball; his addition gave the Grey Sox a solid pitching advantage.

Right: James Patton with the Philadelphia Giants in 1909. *Author's collection.*

Below: James Patton, *seated far right*, with the Philadelphia Giants. *Author's collection.*

Montgomery Grey Sox, 1916. *Back, from left to right*: Marion Cunningham, Horace "Sail Ball Demon" May, unknown, Henry Hannon Jr., unknown, and unknown. *Middle, from left to right*: David "The Great" Cotton, John "Red" Cunningham, Ossie Mitchell (owner), unknown, unknown. *Front*: James Patton and Charleston, catcher. *Courtesy of W.J. Plott.*

James Patton was a well-traveled veteran, having first appeared with Montgomery and Birmingham in the 1890s, as well as the Philadelphia Giants and French Lick Plutos alongside Henry Hannon. Sometimes listed as John, Patton stuck with Montgomery as a player, manager, and coach for many years.

Johnny Goodgame Jr., born in 1894 in Talladega, played with the Chicago Leland Giants and the Brooklyn Giants. In 1911, Goodgame threw a legendary no-hitter for the West Baden Sprudels, defeating the rival French Lick Plutos. Later, John W. Goodgame Jr. would succeed his father as pastor of Birmingham's Sixth Avenue Baptist Church.

The Montgomery Grey Sox finished with a stellar record. Earning three wins over Mobile, taking four of five games from the rival Birmingham Giants, and sweeping the Montgomery Red Sox, the West End Stars, and the Montgomery YMCA, the Grey Sox were absolutely dominant. Montgomery then felled the Pensacola and Evergreen teams before sweeping the Atlanta

Top: John Beckwith, known as "the Brown Bomber," was just sixteen years old when he played for the Montgomery Grey Sox. *Public domain.*

Bottom: McKinley "Bunny" Downs with St. Louis in 1916. *Author's collection.*

Giants to earn an undeniable championship in what was reported as the Colored Southern League of 1915.

By 1916, the Montgomery Grey Sox were widely known as the premier team in the area, winning often enough to claim the title "Champions of the South" and get it in print. The Grey Sox were covered in newspapers across the nation and had continued success drawing large crowds at a time when the white team in town had moved due to poor attendance. The popular lineup featured slugging Henry Hannon, slick-fielding infielder Bunny Downs, the Cunningham brothers, and outfielder/relief pitcher James Patton.

Also on the Grey Sox roster was rookie John Beckwith, acquired during an otherwise dismal northern tour. Just sixteen, the slugging catcher-shortstop would go on to bat .349 over his career and earned the nickname the "Black Bomber" for his prodigious power. The big right-hander stood six-foot-three, weighed 220 pounds, and swung a massive thirty-eight-inch bat with great strength; however, his occasional lackluster attitude and penchant for drink would lessen his effectiveness at times. Playing a long career across three decades, Beckwith is among the all-time leaders in Negro League batting average, home runs, RBIs, and slugging percentage. Of Beckwith, Babe Ruth said, "Not only can Beckwith hit harder than any Negro ballplayer, but any man in the world."

McKinley "Bunny" Downs was young but wasn't a rookie; he had appeared with the West Baden Sprudels and Louisville in 1915 and then joined Montgomery, where he was noted for his hitting and infield skills. Bunny Downs had a long baseball career as a player and manager, later mentoring young Hank Aaron. Downs was later known for signing Mamie "Peanut" Johnson and inserting her in the starting lineup, a move that challenged gender barriers still in place today.

Alphabets and Stars Have Grey Sox Number

The first opponents the Grey Sox faced during the 1916 season were the Indianapolis ABCs, under new manager C.I. Taylor. Taylor's Alphabets proved to be one of the Grey Sox's biggest challenges. Montgomery lost all three hard-fought contests at Tidewater Park in Birmingham. Later, the Grey Sox made a July 4 trip to face Indianapolis, who again swept them.

The Grey Sox also welcomed the Cuban Stars, led by Hall of Famer Cristobal Torriente, who swept the April series. After losing three home games, the Grey Sox and Cubans faced off in Birmingham. Montgomery lost twice more before finally beating ace Eustaquio Pedroso, 6–4.

Teaching a Legend

Notable is a 1914 photo depicting Mount Meigs Juvenile facility students playing baseball with Coach Edward Byrd. Three years later, Byrd taught young Leroy "Satchel" Paige the same game.

Sentenced to Mount Meigs reform school at the age of eleven for shoplifting, Paige spent nearly six years there. Satchel credited Coach

Above: Coach Byrd stands behind the pitcher at a Mount Meigs Juvenile Institute baseball game. *From the National Cyclopedia, 1916, Montgomery Public Library.*

Opposite: Hall of Fame pitcher Satchel Paige was born in Mobile in about 1906. *Public domain.*

Byrd for instructing him to out-think opponents, analyzing hitter stances and bat motions instead of trying to overpower them. Coach Byrd was also credited with creating what became Paige's signature delivery, with high leg kick and arm pulled far behind his back in order to hide the ball from hitters.

Said Paige, "Those five and a half years there did something for me—they made a man out of me....You might say I traded five years of freedom to learn how to pitch."

Wartime Normal School Games

With World War I shutting down even some of the largest leagues in 1917, local league games were few. However, Montgomery's State Normal School baseball team faced opponents such as Howard University and Fiske University at the field on campus. Normal School games often took place at nearby Athletic Park. Some games were at the popular Highland Park Oval, located where Highland Avenue Elementary School now stands, or other smaller fields.

Although Montgomery stars Horace May and Johnny Goodgame were sold to Scranton (Pennsylvania), the Normal School was well stocked with talent, including stars from the Grey Sox. As early as 1905, Grey Sox personnel had appeared as players and umpires for the State Normal School.

In October 1917, the Normal School opposed a team from the 37th Infantry Division's 9th Battalion, comprising African Americans in the Ohio National Guard. It was part of the patriotic wartime support efforts for troops stationed in Montgomery at Camp Sheridan. Located on a vast stretch of Lower Wetumpka Road between Jackson Ferry Road and what is now Maxwell AFB Gunter Annex, Camp Sheridan was the training site for thirty thousand members of Ohio's 37th Infantry "Buckeye" Division. Later these men, including the Black troops, served in France with the 372nd Infantry, earning the Croix de Guerre with Palm for their service amid machine gun and artillery fire at Meuse-Argonne.

As war raged in Europe, for many in Alabama, Black baseball was the only baseball. Montgomery's white pro club moved, unable to draw well

Downtown Montgomery in about 1918, looking southwest. *Author's collection.*

enough to cover payroll. Yet local fans didn't seem to mind, as many had long since shifted to watching Black teams with better players hosting top national competition, often at the same ballparks and for a little less money.

Montgomery Cubs Face Chicago American Giants

The Montgomery Cubs hosted one of the best teams in the nation in 1918: Rube Foster's legendary Chicago American Giants. Manager Foster didn't play himself, but Hall of Famers Pete Hill and Pop Lloyd did. The Chicago Giants shut out the Montgomery Cubs easily, 10–0, behind the pitching of Chicago's ace Dick Whitworth. Horace "Sail Ball Demon" May was the losing pitcher.

Horace "Underhand Sail Ball Demon" May. *Courtesy of W.J. Plott.*

Black Barons and Grey Sox Draw Postwar Crowds

In 1919, the Montgomery Grey Sox and the new Black Barons faced off at Birmingham's Rickwood Field in front of a huge crowd estimated at twelve thousand fans. The doubleheader was one of the largest crowds in the park's long history. George "Tubby" Scales and James Patton pitched for Montgomery, while Marion Cunningham caught both games.

The Grey Sox pitching staff featured Horace "Sail Ball Demon" May, James Patton, and two men only mentioned by last name, Frederick and Madison. Henry Hannon played first base and outfield, with Marion Cunningham handling catching duties. That summer, Cunningham flashed legendary speed as he scored from second base on a sacrifice fly, helping Montgomery win against Birmingham. In August, the Grey Sox handed the Black Crackers their first loss of the season with a stunning ninth-inning rally at Ponce de Leon Park in Atlanta.

The Grey Sox made a very successful road trip early in the season, winning nine of sixteen games against cities "in the north" but ran out of gas by the end of the year. The final series found the Montgomery Grey Sox losing three out of four games to Atlanta, who claimed the league title.

1910–1919 Baseball Across Alabama

The Anniston Giants maintained a strong club and often held big games in Birmingham, using West End Park for contests.

Gadsden, known for fielding a good team, drew many fans when facing clubs in the region. While some opponents such as Macon (Georgia) were well known, others much less so, like the Cave Springs club, who lost three games to the Gadsden team in June 1910. Gadsden also edged the Anniston Giants in a Birmingham series that summer and was said to have lost just two games through midseason.

The Tuscaloosa team held games at their own ballpark in 1911, hosting teams such as the Selma Tigers.

Talladega College had an excellent team in 1911, defeating Selma University, 7–2, behind the pitching of native son Johnny Goodgame. Umpiring the contest was Booker T. Washington Jr.

The Columbia Athletics of Houston County were a strong team in 1912,

BASE-BALL

SELMA TIGERS
VS
TUSCALOOSA GIANTS
Thursday and Friday
Games Called at 4 O'clock At
Colored Baseball Park

The 1911 Tuscaloosa Tigers versus Selma Tigers, advertisement. *Author's collection.*

when they beat Decatur in an August doubleheader. Reports on the Athletics were glowing, with Columbia's star pitcher Mays striking out seventeen hitters as Columbia swept Decatur. Decatur was a tough opponent and known as a "fast" team, having won twenty of twenty-two games in 1912, including two shutouts of Fisk University.

Black women in Alabama were active in playing baseball all across the state. Underwood Park hosted a two-game series between Tuscaloosa and Bessemer's ladies' teams. For twenty-five cents, all were invited to watch the June series in 1912, according to adverts in the *Birmingham News*. Underwood Park is in Birmingham's Southtown neighborhood, close to Five Points South.

Two hundred fans of the Roanoke team made the train ride to LaGrange (Georgia) to see a 1915 game between the two clubs, which Roanoke won 1–0.

The Mobile Athletics included a 1916 stop in Montgomery to face the Grey Sox. Mobile pitcher Hale was among the Athletics best, but he was defeated in that April contest, 13–1.

Birmingham boasted a new city league in 1916. Four clubs—Graymont, the Birmingham Tigers, Edgewater, and Bayview—formed the Jefferson County Colored Baseball Association.

View of Five Points, South Birmingham. *Author's collection.*

Graymont won the title in the league's first season. On the final day of the season, reports from the *Birmingham Post-Herald* listed "Salmon" as the winning pitcher for Edgewater. Harry Salmon, from nearby Warrior, Alabama, would have a long baseball career while working in the coal mines during the offseason.

The Tuskegee team was in court when one of their players, Arthur Smith, scuffled with a porter at Selma's train station. Smith and the porter were both arrested when the team arrived for an April game in 1917. As the fight ensued, the police were swift; the two combatants were immediately hauled before a judge, with the entire Tuskegee team brought as witnesses. Smith was fined five dollars and the porter levied a ten-dollar penalty, as reported by the *Selma Times*.

Birmingham's Tidewater Park was popular for games and events. In August 1917, ACIPCO faced the TCI Ensley Giants as part of Pythian Temple Day festivities. Both ACIPCO's band and the Tuggle Brass Band were on the bill, which featured a parade; admission was twenty-five cents.

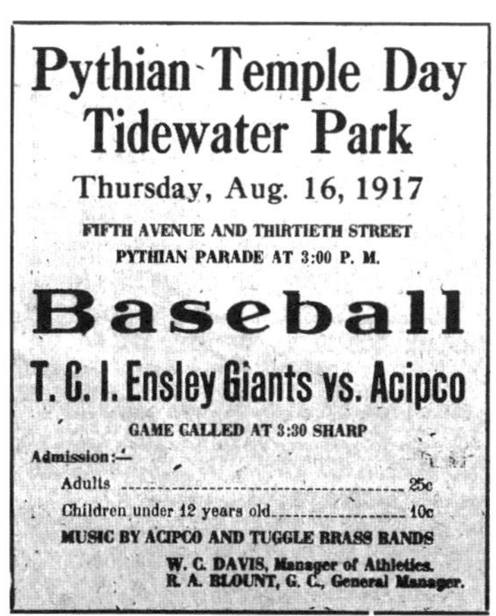

A 1917 advertisement for Pythian Day game featuring Industrial League teams from the *Voice of the People.*

Even smaller cities relied on name recognition. The *Albany-Decatur Daily* covered the 1919 Cedar Lake team of Albany (Alabama) victory over an all-star club from nearby Athens. Cedar Lake, managed by Otis Johnson, claimed three stars on their roster after adding Decatur's top pitcher Fagent to Stover and Humphrey.

Black baseball in Alabama was now a sports-entertainment business. On-field success by teams such as the Birmingham Giants and Montgomery Grey Sox brought new opportunities to the state. Opponents became willing to travel to face talented Alabama teams in new ballparks. Many of them were hiring local players for their own rosters.

Alabama boasted experienced players and front office executives with valuable insight into game management, player development, promotions, and booking contacts. Important connections with men like Rube Foster and the Taylors ushered Alabama into a higher level of play, as well as opening career opportunities and spawning new businesses. In Alabama, players found education and coaching at the highest levels, leading to improved game skills as well as opening other occupational paths. Players began considering Alabama as an athletic career move, creating a deeper pool of talent. As the 1919 season closed, Alabama was budding with baseball ability, booming with new ballparks, and hosting the best teams from the biggest cities in the country.

Bad Bud of Boguehome

His mother Sallie (with an "ie") called him Jimmie (with an "ie"), but everyone in Boguehome knew him as Bud. Bud was what Negro Leaguers called a "hard case," someone into wild living and possessing a harsh attitude or mean spirit. Late nights of booze, gambling, and fast women were definitely in Bud's repertoire; he was well known in the night spots around town, as well as at City Court.

Bud's adventures often involved gambling. In one instance, Bud was caught running a skin game. When police apprehended the group of suspected gamblers, the other men were penniless, but when Bud was shaken down, he was found carrying more than eighty dollars in small bills and loose change.

A few times, Bud appeared in court on charges of carrying a concealed pistol. After a guilty plea, he paid the fine, ten dollars for the first offense. Then twenty bucks. Then thirty. Bud was once accused of swindling someone out of fourteen dollars. Another time, Bud was among a group of men busted playing craps, and later he was arrested for vagrancy. It was a bum rap, they said—Bud never had any trouble paying. He was a man of means.

For a time, Bud worked as a bartender in a Decatur Avenue saloon. Unfortunately, he and another barkeep were found siphoning booze from their stocks. Police were sure that the pair had been bootlegging large quantities but could only charge them for the small amount found on them at the time of the arrest. Being caught with a few pints earned Bud a small fine. He paid it easily.

Then Bud was caught up in an illegal meat distribution scheme, involved in selling uninspected raw meats to local grocers. Bud's role was never fully discerned, and he was released after questioning.

Bud was with his pal Sam Watson and a woman named Belle Austin one evening when the three of them attempted a late-night entry into a Decatur Street store. The shopkeeper, Willie Page, was ready, as someone had tipped him off about the break-in, and Willie waited with his shotgun. The sound of the blast brought a passing police foot patrol bursting through the front door almost immediately. Officers found Belle Austin dead on the floor as Bud and Sam beat a hasty escape. Bud and Sam were quickly caught but released. Only shopkeeper Willie Page was charged in the shooting of Belle Austin.

Bud was once accused of running a bunco scheme, working with a notorious thug to rob unsuspecting train travelers. The victim would be hit over the head and relieved of their valuables as the bandits exited the train as it stopped. The case was flimsy due to lack of evidence, and Bud was released.

And there was the time Bud shot and killed Gus Moten at the picnic in White Hall, near Hayneville. He turned himself in and was released on his own recognizance. And then he was released again following the hearing.

One evening in Boguehome, Bud's brother Morris went to meet Bud at the corner of South Street and Decatur Avenue, where he saw a white man beating Bud severely while bystanders gawked. Morris, who carried a pistol, pulled his weapon and fired twice. The attacker dropped to the street, dead from a bullet to the chest.

Officers arrived quickly. The brothers and several others standing nearby were arrested on the spot. Morris admitted that he shot the man and surrendered his weapon. Bud was also armed, and his gun was confiscated.

The victim, David Thurman, was a deputized constable serving subpoenas for the sheriff's office, tasked with looking for a man. However, Thurman, drunk when killed, was found with a bottle of liquor and had a public disagreement with Bud at a dance hall before the shooting. The witnesses confirmed the story and corroborated Morris's admission. Yet officials were not convinced. Both Morris and Bud were held while Montgomery's coroner examined the corpse of the victim. Morris was carrying a .38-caliber pistol; the police thought that the large chest wound on their constable resembled a .45-caliber injury. Bud carried a .45.

On examination of the body, the fatal bullet was indeed noted to be a .38-caliber slug. Bud was released following Morris's proven confession.

The following day, Bud was arrested again for the killing when Montgomery police received telegrams stating that there was proof of Bud's guilt. A lawyer named Fuller, a judge's son, lurked about the city jail that afternoon until he found his chance to push past the sentries. Rushing to Bud's cell, the young Fuller pulled a pistol and fired one shot at Bud before jailers intervened. Bud was unhurt, as Fuller's shot missed its mark. Bud's cellmate was struck and badly wounded. Fuller's father, Judge Fuller, condemned the shooting and announced that he would have his son declared insane and institutionalized.

It was learned that the young Fuller was the brother-in-law of the deceased constable and sent the telegrams falsely accusing Bud. Witnesses came forward who heard young Fuller make death threats involving Bud, as there was a long-standing dispute between the two. Bud was released again.

Morris and Bud were exonerated when a grand jury declared the use of force justified, and the murder charges were dismissed. Morris was fined $400 for carrying a concealed weapon, equivalent to more than $12,000 by modern standards. He paid in cash. Another concealed weapon charge a few weeks later got Morris six months of hard labor.

Eighteen months later, at about 9:00 p.m. on a December evening, Bud was walking out of his favorite Boguehome saloon at the corner of South and Decatur Streets when he was shot by a young street tough named George Edward. Bud took two bullets to the chest, dying the next day. Edward fled the scene but was caught, convicted of manslaughter, and sentenced to one year of hard labor. Newspapers said that James "Bud" Hannon was "known to be a desperate character" in town.

Hearing of Bud's death and now the eldest brother of the family, Bud's brother Henry rushed home from his job in Indiana. Henry had been playing professional baseball with the French Lick Plutos. Henry Hannon Jr., backed by his father Henry Sr., would reorganize James's old-time Greys/Blues team as the Montgomery Grey Sox within a year.

CHAPTER 7

1920s MONTGOMERY'S GREY SOX

The Negro Southern League (NSL) was created in 1920 in connection with the Negro National League (NNL), among the top levels of organized baseball. Rosters were normalized, and statistics and cumulative standings were recorded. Alabama earned two entries, Birmingham and Montgomery. The Montgomery Grey Sox had established a reputation for being among the best teams in Alabama, earning an invitation to the newly forged circuit.

The Grey Sox quickly moved to the top of the NSL standings, bolstered with the additions of Sam Streeter, Deacon Meyers, and Jim Moss to the pitching staff. The lineup was powerful, backed by hard-hitting Tubby Scales and the speedy Cunningham brothers. The competition was top level. In a game hosting Indianapolis, future Hall of Famer Oscar Charleston hit a home run that cleared the fence at Montgomery's League Park at Highland Oval, well over five hundred feet.

John Staples, an African American storeowner and entrepreneur with a popular Cleveland Avenue grocery store, had played with Montgomery's team. Staples handled bookings, promotions, and front office tasks. He was instrumental in the creation of a new ballpark as part of an entertainment complex on Holt Street. The innovative Staples employed a large jazz band to entertain at Grey Sox games, creating a lively atmosphere that often drew more than one thousand fans per day. Some games were held at Athletic Park in Boguehome or Highland Oval near Oak Park.

Montgomery Grey Sox, 1920. *Back, from left to right*: Hub McGavock, Jim Hugh Moss, James Patton, Mr. Pigler, John Staples, Two Sides Wesley, Bob McCormack, Deacon Myers, and Big Mason. *Front, from left to right*: Poindexter Williams, Marion Cunningham, Preston, Sam Streeter, George Scales, Herman Cunningham, and Clay Carpenter. *Courtesy of W.J. Plott.*

Staples sometimes served as umpire, but any doubts about his fairness dissipated when he ejected one of his own Grey Sox players from a game for arguing with his calls. Staples also employed former players such as Horace May and David Cotton as umpires.

THE CUNNINGHAM FAMILY

Brothers Marion "Dad" Cunningham, Herman "Rounders" Cunningham, and John "Red" Cunningham are three of the most popular players in Montgomery's baseball history. Beginning around 1910, the Cunningham family name appears with a variety of local and national teams before combining in Montgomery to lift their hometown Grey Sox to new heights.

Marion Cunningham, well known for a reliable glove as well as strong hitting, played first base or catcher and was the team manager. Known as "Dad" or sometimes "Red," Marion Cunningham was widely considered Montgomery's top infielder during his career. A lifelong Montgomery resident,

Left: Marion Cunningham. *Middle*: Herman Cunningham. *Right*: John Cunningham. *Courtesy of W.J. Plott.*

Marion Cunningham worked with the L&N Railroad in Montgomery and served in World War I. With the Grey Sox, Marion was a defensive wizard in the field and made consistent contact at the plate.

Slick-fielding Herman Cunningham often played shortstop on the Grey Sox infield. Herman appeared in many of the biggest Grey Sox games. A clutch hitter and solid defender, he was the youngest of the brothers.

The eldest, John "Red" Cunningham, four years older than Marion with whom he sometimes shared a nickname, was a veteran presence, having played on C.I. Taylor's French Lick Plutos. John's slick fielding and steady hitting helped fill the Grey Sox lineup with top-shelf ability. More than forty years after his playing days, Red was still recalled as an unequalled star, a natural showman who could "do everything with a baseball as well as hit it a country mile."

The Cunningham family home on Mill Street was just blocks from South Side Park in the Washington Park neighborhood. Previously, the Cunninghams lived on South Jackson Street in the Centennial Hill area near the State Normal School. The proximity to nearby ballparks was no coincidence, as the Cunningham's remained close to the game through the mid-1980s.

HANNON, SCALES, AND TWO SIDES LEAD GREY SOX OFFENSE

This page, top: Henry Hannon Jr., 1916. *Courtesy of W.J. Plott.*

This page, bottom: George Scales at Ponce de Leon, 1944. *Author's collection.*

Opposite, top: Talladega native George "Tubby" Scales with Montgomery. *Courtesy of Bill Plott.*

Opposite, bottom: Charlie "Two Sides" Wesley, 1920 Grey Sox. *Courtesy of W.J. Plott.*

An integral part of Montgomery's baseball, Henry Hannon Jr., born in 1882 in Montgomery, had already appeared with the Cuban Giants, St. Louis Stars, Chicago Giants, and French Lick Plutos. He played in the legendary no-hitter between the French Lick Plutos and West Baden Sprudels in 1911 that connected many Alabama players.

Credited with fewer than forty games officially, Hannon played in hundreds of contests, managing many more as a pioneer of baseball with the Montgomery Grey Sox. His father, Henry Sr., had long been connected to Montgomery baseball and continued to finance the team. Henry's elder brother James "Bud" Hannon had been an outfielder for many years. Henry Jr. ran a Decatur Street fish shop when not playing baseball.

Montgomery was bolstered by hard-hitting George "Tubby" Scales. Scales's arrival coincided with the team's rise in popularity and on-field success. Along with Streeter, Hannon, and the Cunninghams, they formed a strong lineup. Scales, a slugging power hitter who could play any position with ease, also pitched occasionally. The career of Scales, a Talladega native, was a long one, continuing as a player until age forty-five. He appeared with and managed teams such as the New York Lincoln Giants and Homestead Grays and also found success in Puerto Rico, where he won six pennants as a player/manager.

Joining Montgomery after starring for the Tuskegee college team while still attending high school, Scales was a big bat in the Grey Sox lineup. With a career batting average of .319, Scales played fourteen consecutive seasons without batting below .300 and twice topped the .400 mark. Currently, Scales leads all HOF-eligible Negro Leaguers in batting average, on base

percentage, and slugging percentage and is sixth among eligible Negro League position players in WAR. His slugging percentage ranks ninth among the top ten Negro Leaguers; the eight above him are enshrined in Cooperstown.

Since 2000, Scales has twice been considered for Baseball's Hall of Fame at Cooperstown, most recently in 2022 by the Early Days Committee, receiving eight of the necessary twelve votes. He is long regarded as one of the greats of the game, and many feel that the only question about George Scales's call to the Hall of Fame is simply when it will happen.

Montgomery native Charles "Two Sides" Wesley was a huge part of the Grey Sox success, playing nearly every game at second base or in the outfield. The talented and popular "Two Sides" also featured with the Birmingham Black Barons and other teams during his long, successful baseball career. In 1924, Wesley married famous blues singer Clara Smith, who had mentored actress Josephine Baker.

Pitching Strengths: Deacon and Streeter

The depth of Montgomery's pitching staff was among the team's strengths. Strong pitching from youngster George "Deacon" Meyers, just nineteen years old when he arrived in Montgomery, helped solidify the club with consistent mound work. After his success with Montgomery, Meyers went on to join St. Louis. He would easily have been the Grey Sox's top starter had it not been for Sam Streeter.

Montgomery's ace was undoubtedly Sam Streeter, whose work with the Grey Sox became the stuff of legend. Sam "Lefty" Streeter, a Madison County native, was known for missing bats with his wide sweeping curve and baffling spitball.

Later, Streeter would start the first East-West All-Star Game in 1933. He handily defeated teams of white all-stars in exhibition games. Hall of

Far left: Deacon Meyers, 1920 Grey Sox. *Courtesy of W.J. Plott.*

Left: Sam Streeter, 1920 Grey Sox. *Courtesy of W.J. Plott.*

Opposite: The 1920 Grey Sox versus the Atlanta Black Crackers, advertisement. *Author's collection.*

Fame catcher Josh Gibson called Sam the smartest pitcher in the league. With Montgomery's Grey Sox, Sam Streeter set records that still stand and authored some of the most dominant pitching performances in the city's history.

On June 7, 1920, Montgomery's Sam Streeter pitched a game against the Birmingham Black Barons that was remembered as the longest scoreless inning streak by one pitcher in one game in Rickwood Field history. Streeter threw fifteen scoreless innings before taking the loss in the sixteenth inning due to fielding errors.

The barnstorming Chicago Black Sox were soundly defeated by Montgomery in a July 22 game widely attended by local fans. Already excited about the prospect of a Grey Sox pennant, the large crowd was thrilled as Grey Sox hurler Sam Streeter dealt twenty consecutive pitches for strikes without contact. He allowed just four hits and earned the victory.

STREETER'S PERFECT GAME

Less than a week later, on July 27, Montgomery Grey Sox pitcher Sam "Lefty" Streeter was perfect, tossing the first Montgomery Grey Sox no-hitter in a game against the Black Crackers in Atlanta, winning 3–0 in the first game of a doubleheader. Not a single Black Cracker reached first base. The Grey Sox took both games when Montgomery starter Deacon Meyers earned the win for the Sox in the nightcap.

BASE BALL
TOMORROW
MONTGOMERY GREY SOX
VS.
ATLANTA BLACK CRACKERS
South Side Park.
Game called at 4 o'clock.

Streeter tossed several other gems, including an August one-hitter against Birmingham. Streeter was one of the most dominant pitchers of the Negro Southern League in 1920, officially credited with winning fifteen games and completing twenty-five of his starting assignments.

Grey Sox Named 1920 NSL Champions Amid Controversy

Montgomery won forty-eight and lost forty league games during the season, sometimes hosting more than three thousand fans per game. Yet the Negro Southern League was not without issues. Among the recurring problems in the front office was a lack of official standings. League offices were sporadically sent game reports by teams, with some being categorized as league games and others as exhibitions, leading to discrepancies. Some teams were prompt in reporting their game results, while others were very tardy. As a result, the league mandated a late-season scheduling change forcing teams to adjust to accommodate Knoxville's missing more than a dozen league contests while suddenly claiming extra victories, resulting in league-wide protests.

At the end of the season, the Knoxville Giants, with a higher winning percentage but fewer total wins, were chosen to represent the Negro Southern League in the playoffs against Chicago's American Giants, who dominated the three-game series. The Grey Sox still faced Chicago in an exhibition series, as the stadium was already booked. Billed as a Championship Series, Montgomery was beaten in two of three games by the Giants.

The day after the series, the Montgomery Grey Sox won the Negro Southern League pennant for 1920. League president Perdue disallowed some of Knoxville's contested games due to ineligible players on their roster, declaring Montgomery champions. To this day, Knoxville and Montgomery both claim the 1920 NSL pennant.

1921: GREY SOX OFF AND RUNNING WITH TURKEY AND HUB

James "Doc" Patton was replaced as manager, with David "The Great" Cotton taking over. The core of the team returned in the form of the Cunningham brothers, and the club made some key acquisitions. Pitcher Slim Sallee and slugger Hub McGavock were big producers for the Grey Sox this season. Scales and Streeter moved on; Deacon Meyers remained to anchor the pitching staff with Mason.

In March, the Champion Grey Sox were big news with a rare write-up in the *Montgomery Advertiser* that covered player names and their positions and even included the team's schedule. The Grey Sox home opener featured the team hoisting the Negro Southern League 1920 championship flag. Reverend Stokes threw out the first pitch, and Montgomery held the Black Barons to just three hits in a thrilling 2–1 victory.

Norman "Turkey" Stearnes had one of the most unorthodox batting stances in baseball yet became the Negro League's career home run leader. *Author's collection, public domain.*

On opening day against the Black Barons, "Stern" was listed as the leadoff hitter, getting one hit. On May 21, future Baseball Hall of Famer Norman "Turkey" Stearnes rapped another hit as Montgomery beat the New Orleans Caulfields. These are among the first documented games with Montgomery for Turkey Stearnes, set on a path to Cooperstown.

By the time Norman Stearnes was selected to become a Hall of Famer in the year 2000, Alabama's fans had long recognized him as a patron of baseball history and for his connection with the Grey Sox dynasty. They weren't alone, as Hall of Famer Cool

Papa Bell was quoted saying, "If they don't put Turkey Stearnes in the Hall of Fame, they shouldn't put anybody!"

A five-time All-Star who won two batting titles, "Turkey" Stearnes's connection with Alabama has become one of myth as much as fact. Few local fans realize that Stearnes is not from Alabama, as official press releases often repeated the claim that Turkey Stearnes started with Montgomery. Birmingham has also called him a "hometown" product. Perhaps fans held on to the memory of his big hits that aided the popular Montgomery Grey Sox. Perhaps they were taken with Stearnes's youthful energy or endeared by the way he ran while wildly flapping his elbows like wings. Whatever the reason, Alabama baseball fans warmly embraced Turkey Stearnes and never let go.

Born in Nashville in 1901, Norman Stearnes claimed that he got his nickname "Turkey" as a youth. In a 1940 interview in *The Call* of Kansas City, Stearnes was quoted, "When I was a kid I was all chest, no hips and no legs. So the boys on the team thought upon Turkey as the nickname and it has stuck with me ever since." Others said that it was his habit of running with his elbows askew that earned him the moniker by which he would be known. The swift-fielding, strong-armed power hitter first played with Nashville as an eighteen-year-old, batting .265 as a rookie and making most of his appearances as a pitcher.

Stearnes had pitched in high school, tossing two shutouts before earning a spot with the Nashville Giants, where Montgomery owner John Staples found him. Staples had to ask Stearnes's mother's permission to bring the youngster to play with the Grey Sox. Stearnes said that he developed a "cold in his arm" upon arriving at Montgomery, but his strong bat kept him off the bench. Turkey Stearnes was clutch for Montgomery and quickly found himself as the starting centerfielder for a Grey Sox team chasing a playoff spot. Records for individuals are spotty. Stearns is "officially" credited with eighteen at-bats and one home run with Montgomery in 1921. That home run was likely the first of his career; when he finally hung up his spikes, he did so as the all-time career leader in Negro League home runs with 183 long balls.

Stearnes's batting stance was even more unorthodox than his base running. The left-handed hitter would strike an unusual pose in the batter's box, swinging from what is today called a "wide open" stance. It was almost unheard of in that era for a batter to stand with his hips and shoulders facing the pitcher, yet Turkey Stearnes's batting style had many more quirks.

The 1927 Philadelphia Royal Giants with Willie Foster, *far left*, and Norman "Turkey" Stearnes, *second from left. Author's collection, public domain.*

Turkey would stand in his wide-open stance, facing the pitcher, and set up for each pitch by pointing the end of his bat straight up toward the sky, with the knob over home plate, fully extending both of his long arms straight forward. Then he'd slowly lean the top of the bat toward the pitcher. Finally, as the pitcher began his delivery, Stearnes would dig his right heel in the dirt, pointing his toes up toward the sky.

On Turkey Stearnes's batting stance, Hall of Fame pitcher Satchel Paige said he "hit with his right foot in the bucket and twisted his right heel and pointed his big toe up." Satchel knew Stearnes's stance well, as Paige once gave up hits in six consecutive at-bats to Stearnes. On the seventh time facing Stearnes, Satchel rolled the ball along the ground to the plate, shouting, "Let's see you hit that one!"

Stearnes's stance may have been one of the most bizarre to ever step into any batter's box, yet his blazing base running speed and ability to make solid contact lifted his career batting average to an elite .348 mark, seventh highest in major-league history. Turkey Stearnes's career slugging percentage (.6157) is fifth all-time among all major leaguers.

Over his twenty-year career, Turkey Stearnes averaged one home run every sixteen at-bats, on par with Hank Aaron and Lou Gehrig, ranking among the top home run hitters in all of baseball history. As a young outfielder, Willie Mays often heard comparisons of Stearnes's defensive abilities from longtime Negro League observers. Alabama's fans certainly never forgot the Hall of Famer called Turkey.

Herbert Thornton McGavock, known as "Hub," was born in 1896 near Nashville, Tennessee. The slugging outfielder's career is often "officially" listed with the Indianapolis ABC's in 1919 and little else. Hub McGavock played for teams in and around Nashville following an Army stint during

Herbert "Hub" McGavock with Baltimore, from the *Nashville Globe*, 1916.

World War I. Upon his return from service, he joined Turkey Stearnes on the Nashville Standard Giants. In Montgomery, he reunited with Stearnes as teammates.

McGavock was a reliable outfielder and clutch bat, highlighted often for his hitting and glove. Patrolling left field for Montgomery, he was known for a cannon throwing arm, in one game cutting down two runners at home plate. Like many players at the time, his strong arm sometimes found him working on the mound, but his pitching lacked finesse and he was more often utilized afield.

Deacon Meyers and Slim Sallee Twirl No-Hit Gems

On May 8, 1921, Grey Sox starting pitcher Deacon Meyers tossed the second of Montgomery's Negro Southern League no-hit games, blanking the Knoxville Giants, 18–0.

Just two days later, on May 10, Grey Sox pitcher Slim Sallee no-hit Knoxville as Montgomery won 6–0 in a seven-inning game. With no other information on anyone named Sallee, it appears that someone played incognito, having "borrowed" the name of the well-known white lefty pitcher with the Cincinnati Reds, etching their pseudonym in the record books.

The Grey Sox made midseason moves to strengthen the pitching staff, including adding the dominant hurler "Steel Arm" Dickey during his incredible streak of twenty consecutive victories. With the addition of Dickey, the Grey Sox had the authors of four no-hit games on their staff, as Steel Arm had thrown two of the rare gems the previous season.

Grey Sox Involved in Pennant Flap, Postseason Flop

Winning sixty-nine games and losing fifty for a winning percentage of .580, the Grey Sox had a second place showing in 1921. Or possibly higher, as the *Montgomery Advertiser* reported eighty wins and proclaimed them NSL Champions. Nashville, with seventy-two victories, disputed the claim.

Complicated by the lack of accurate reporting, teams that failed to complete their schedule, and being unable to differentiate between league games and barnstorming/exhibition box scores, historians are unable to determine the actual standings. The same problem may have confronted the Negro Southern League front office. After being denied a postseason opportunity due to similar schedule shenanigans the previous season, Montgomery was chosen for the playoffs against the Negro National League.

Montgomery's Grey Sox were poised for playoff greatness, scheduled for a twelve-game/three-city road trip and a chance to become the best team in the Negro Leagues. The club was due to visit St. Louis and Chicago for a three-team playoff series followed by a stop in Nashville advertised as the NSL Championship. It was a golden opportunity for Henry Hannon's Grey Sox to claim the biggest prize in Negro League baseball, a world championship.

In St. Louis, Montgomery was opposed by former Grey Sox third baseman Tubby Scales, now with the Giants. The powerful St. Louis Giants overwhelmed them in four of the five games. Hall of Famer Oscar Charleston of St. Louis had a huge series to cap off his most historic season. Montgomery's Steel Arm Dickey picked up the lone Grey Sox victory.

The Grey Sox packed their grip and rode to Chicago, where they lost two tight games, swept by Rube Foster's mighty Chicago American Giants. Montgomery's Steel Arm Dickey struck out nine men and gave up only four hits and a walk, losing a heartbreaker when the Giants scored on two ninth-inning errors.

The Montgomery Grey Sox were then beaten four games to one by Nashville. After winning the season pennant with eighty victories, the Grey Sox managed just two wins in twelve postseason games.

1922: Stringbean and Wing

Spring announcements informed fans of the Grey Sox roster with N.E. Abercrombie as president. He had previously handled that role as early as 1897. Nicholas Abercrombie Jr. graduated Tuskegee University in 1888, was appointed to the post office in Montgomery in 1892, and served with distinction for more than forty years. Abercrombie's father,

Top: Andrew "String Bean" Williams was thirty-six years old in his first known season with West Baden's Sprudels, yet his baseball career continued for another sixteen years. *Author's collection, public domain.*

Bottom: Forrest "One-Wing" Maddox was one of the most popular players in the South. *Dr. Layton Revel/Negro Southern League Museum.*

Nick Sr., was famously connected. The elder Abercrombie arrived in Montgomery before the Civil War and was a popular barber who had friendships with many influential clients, including presidents, generals, governors, and society elites.

The Montgomery lineup included "Turkey" Stearnes and the Cunningham brothers and featured a strong pitching staff comprising James Moss, "Big" Mason, and two wildly popular veterans, "One-Wing" Maddox and a curious journeyman named Williams.

Andrew "String Bean" Williams, an effective submarine-style pitcher, was more than the average veteran. String Bean's long career is often considered the prototype for Satchel Paige.

Born in 1873, Andrew Williams was forty-nine years old when he took the mound for Montgomery, where many of his Grey Sox teammates were less than half his age. One year later, at the age of fifty, Williams pitched with the Brooklyn Royal Giants in what is regarded as the oldest major-league debut in history. However, that was Williams's second stint with Brooklyn, as he had pitched for them six full years earlier, before the league organized.

Williams was among only a handful of Negro Leaguers known to have served in the Spanish-American War, another being C.I. Taylor. "String Bean" had many connections to Montgomery; he had pitched with the West Baden Sprudels and was often on Taylor-run teams. Williams and Henry Hannon had both appeared with Rube Foster's Louisville club, and String Bean had been teammates with infielder Bunny Downs in St. Louis.

Forrest "Wing" Maddox was a popular addition to the Grey Sox. The one-armed pitcher/outfielder was in high demand across the South for his drawing power, dazzling with his ability and charismatic presence on the field. After losing his left arm in an accident at the age of ten, Maddox was forced to find his own unique style. The *Birmingham News* called Maddox a "Houdini" for his spectacular outfield defensive ability.

Forrest Maddox starred at Morehouse University as a two-way player and then played with Atlanta, Knoxville, and Birmingham's Black Barons. Maddox built a reputation as a pretty good pitcher and excellent contact hitter, becoming a fan favorite everywhere he played.

Grey Sox Fade

The Grey Sox played well but faded, winning seventeen and losing eleven in official league games. Or possibly twenty-nine wins and thirty-eight losses, as reported by the *Nashville Banner*. As in many NSL seasons, the total number of wins in the league doesn't match the total number of losses reported, casting doubt on the actual standings. The Grey Sox boasted a winning record for the first half but slumped badly afterward. It wasn't just a local problem; nationwide Prohibition and other issues were taking their toll, and the NSL essentially folded at the start of August. As the team slipped in the standings, they slipped from the newspaper columns until after the season, when tragedy struck.

Grey Sox Torn Apart by Killings

In November 1922, John Cunningham was killed, shot by a white store owner in a late-night "confusion" on the sidewalk in front of a shop at 806 Decatur Street in Boguehome. Fatally wounded, John Cunningham was taken to Hale Infirmary, where he died from his injuries. Newspapers offer few details about the events that led to the tragic killing yet unanimously hailed Cunningham as a baseball star widely respected for his stellar Grey Sox play.

The man who shot Cunningham, Tom Farmer, was arrested and charged, but he was acquitted in the killing when his self-defense plea was accepted for shooting John Cunningham twice in the back. As a result, Farmer walked free.

Killing John Cunningham was not Tom Farmer's first shooting. He shot and wounded a burglar breaking into his home in 1914. Three years later, Farmer was arrested for shooting a Black man named Willie Harris just one block from where Farmer would later shoot Cunningham. When Harris recovered, the charges were dropped.

Farmer's Boguehome house was raided in 1921. He was arrested and fined for possessing bootleg booze. Just six months later, Farmer was back in court for brutally attacking a Black man with an axe handle. That attack occurred just six months before the tragic shooting of John Cunningham. Following his acquittal for killing Cunningham, Farmer retreated to his family's country home, where he was injured in a gory lumber saw accident.

John Cunningham's death was the first in a series of deadly tragedies that befell the Grey Sox.

Just months after John Cunningham's killing, pitcher Steel Arm Dickey was in a brawl sparked over moonshine; his throat was cut by a white man.

Claude "Steel Arm" Dickey was in his hometown of Etowah, Tennessee, in March 1923, standing on a street corner with four other men when they encountered twenty-seven-year-old Waldo Keys. What happened next depends on which newspapers you believe.

According to the *Chattanooga Times*, Dickey and his group approached Waldo and demanded he buy moonshine from them. Waldo Keys said that he refused, saying he had no money, but when it became apparent that he did have cash, he was attacked. Waldo said that he was knocked down twice before he managed to get to his pocketknife and slash his way out of the melee. He dashed from the attackers and jumped onto the running board of a passing car, escaping with three broken ribs.

With two-no hitters and a twenty-game win streak, Claude "Steel Arm" Dickey was the top pitcher in the early NSL. *Dr. Layton Revel/Negro Southern League Museum.*

Reports in the *Chicago Defender* tell a much different story of Waldo Keys meeting Claude Dickey. In this version, Waldo entered the Jim Crow section of Etowah with a carload of white associates. Waldo Keys's group waved cash and demanded bootleg booze from the men standing on the street corner. Dickey and the others refused, telling them that they had no liquor. Waldo Keys became enraged and attacked the group of men. After viciously wounding multiple victims, Keys jumped into the car with the other white men, driving pell-mell for the state line.

Regardless of which version is closer to the actual facts, the results were the same—and they were fatal. Claude Dickey was injured in the neck and died from loss of blood. Coroner reports, which confusingly listed him as "Walter Dickey," indicated a gunshot wound as the cause of death, but newspapers consistently stated that Dickey was killed when Waldo Keys slashed him with a knife. "Cool Papa" Bell, speaking much later, mentioned that missing bootlegging profits may have sparked the dispute.

1923: Grey Sox Hung Out to Dry

In 1923, Grey Sox stars Sam Streeter and Two Sides Wesley joined Birmingham's Black Barons. The NSL reorganized, but Montgomery was left out of the circuit. With no reason offered publicly, it's possible that the team was unwilling or unable to replace John Cunningham. Finances were also a factor, as the Grey Sox had been rapidly selling players, indicating that times were tight for ownership. The situation worsened when in November 1922, Henry Hannon Sr., who funded the team, was crushed to death at his job in a Birmingham railyard, leaving the team without its backer. In April, Henry Jr's youngest brother, Calvin, died in a Montgomery shooting.

A box score for a June game between the Pensacola Giants and the Montgomery All-Stars appeared in the *Pensacola News* but offered few clues about the players involved.

News was sparse, but the *Baltimore Afro-American* mentioned the Alabama State Hornets team playing against the Grey Sox in April 1924. There was also a *Montgomery Times* report of the Grey Sox hosting Pensacola for a July 4 doubleheader.

In 1925, the Sox continued to lay low. Newspapers occasionally mentioned the Grey Sox hosting Pensacola's Giants and on the road against Atlanta's Black Crackers in 1925. One trip to Atlanta resulted in a 10–0 rain-shortened loss to the Black Crackers. However, Montgomery minimized the damage by signing a pair of Atlanta players to bolster their roster.

Ben Mollette was reported as umpiring Grey Sox games this season. He was a longtime Montgomery umpire, and his relationship to Montgomery's 1890s pitcher Oscar "Hawk" Molette is unknown but conspicuous.

1926: Refurbished Grey Sox Return

The NSL was reorganized, with Henry Hannon appointed as league secretary. Montgomery's business manager H.J. Bailey represented them at league meetings. Bailey owned a shoe repair shop at 116 North Court Street. In 1920, Bailey purchased a luxury seven-passenger auto and started the first Black-owned taxi service in Montgomery; he later ran a popular café.

Team president John Samuels operated a neighborhood grocery store near Oak Park. In 1902, in another action that foreshadowed future civil rights efforts, John Samuels was the very first person arrested for refusing to move to the back of a Montgomery streetcar, defying new Jim Crow laws.

Henry Hannon was managing, and popular Forrest "One Wing" Maddox was back to lead the pitching staff. The Grey Sox played at North Side Park at the former site of Camp Sheridan,

Left: William Burns Anderson. *Alabama State University.*

Below: A 1916 advertisement for H.J. Bailey's store in the *Montgomery Advertiser.*

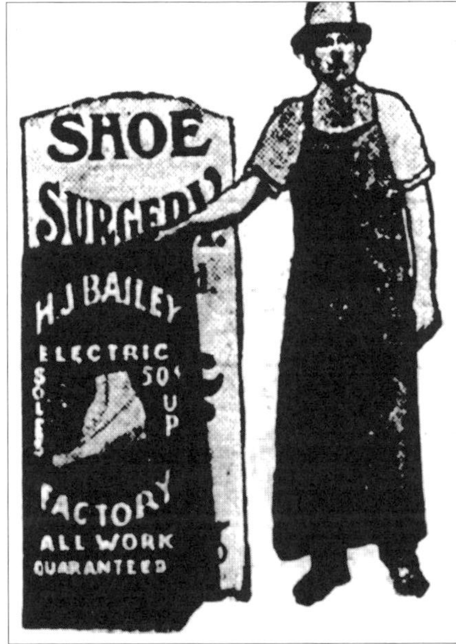

A Song Worth While

Same old place and same old price,
Get work quick and get work nice
Never too soon and never too late,
To get work done and while you wait.
Very best leather and very best heel,
Give you rubber or give you steel.
Half soles sewed or half soles nailed,
All done right—I never have failed.
And if by chance a fault you find,
Bring it right back, and I don't mind
To satisfy you for that's my job—
To please my friends, and not to rob.
If you have a job you want right away,
Just ring 3165-J.

Alabama Electric Shoe Repairing Factory

H. J. BAILEY, Prop.
Phone 3165-J.
116 North Court St. Montgomery, Ala.

as well as South Side Park and Athletic Park/Alabama State, where players like Bill Anderson were scouted.

Grey Sox rookie Bill Anderson, a student at the State Teachers College, was just nineteen years old. William "Bill" Anderson's life was tragically cut short at the young age of twenty-five while working as a teacher in Northport, Alabama, on March 21, 1932, during a deadly tornado outbreak that struck the Midwest and southern United States. The two-day "super-tornado" event caused 268 fatalities and destroyed thousands of homes and was the deadliest tornado outbreak in Alabama history.

Thou Shalt Not Steal

The *Nashville Tennessean* mentioned the Grey Sox flair for the dramatic when Montgomery's catcher, Molder, was reported wearing a chest protector on which was boldly written "Thou Shalt Not Steal." In April 1926, the Montgomery Grey Sox hosted the legendary Cuban Stars. The Cuban Stars East featured Hall of Famer Martin Dhigio and other Cuban greats but were beaten in two of three games by the Grey Sox.

Grey Sox Unravel After Selling Satchel

Pitching in relief for the Chattanooga White Sox, Satchel Paige, the star of the Chattanooga staff, was pressed into duty in Montgomery when the first two hurlers were ineffective on July 25. The following day, the Sox paired up again, with Satchel starting for Chattanooga. The teams traded runs often, and the score stood at six apiece by the end of nine innings. Chattanooga scored twice in the tenth, and Satchel surrendered a solo homer and then set down the Grey Sox to earn the win. Interviewed later, Montgomery veterans said that the rookie Paige had been signed by Montgomery in spring but was sold to Chattanooga before the season.

A filing on July 22 showed the Montgomery Grey Sox acquiring midseason capital when the ownership group added A.E. Wells. A prominent white businessman from Birmingham and owner of Wells Furniture, Wells infused the team with $1,800 cash. The Grey Sox then failed to appear for an August game in Chattanooga, reportedly due to an auto accident.

They were replaced on the league schedule, and nothing more is known of the team this season. Montgomery's Grey Sox were officially 22-40, well out of contention.

Following the season, in November, team president John Samuels passed away at his home on Seay Street, leaving another void in the Grey Sox front office.

In 1927, the Bessemer Grey Sox, also called the Cunningham Grey Sox by the *Birmingham Reporter*, held a lesser, associate member spot in the Negro Southern League. The next year, the Atlanta team adopted the name and for two seasons were the Atlanta Grey Sox.

James Moss Doomed by Phrenology

In 1927, former Montgomery pitcher Jim Moss was with a white couple in a car loaded with bootlegged moonshine. The couple, Clifford Thompson and his wife, Eula, stopped at a general store in Chatsworth, Georgia, with Moss in tow. At the store, owned by Mr. Coleman Osborne, someone from the car produced a firearm and murdered Osborne. The trio were arrested, quickly tried, and easily convicted. All three were sentenced to the Georgia electric chair.

James Moss was listed variously as Jim Moss, James Hughbert Moss, Jim Hugh Moss, or often just "Moss," and many details about this pitcher's career on the field are still shrouded in mystery. Born in June 1897 in Tennessee, James Moss and pitcher "Steel Arm" Dickey were both residents of Etowah, Tennessee, and rumored to be involved in bootlegging. Moss listed L&N Railroad as his employer and was married, with at least two and possibly as many as five children. Moss may have first played pro ball in Chicago before turning up in 1919 with the barnstorming Fast Havana Stars (with no Cuban connections). Moss appeared with Montgomery as an outfielder and pitcher in 1920 and again in '22.

James Moss, 1920 Montgomery Grey Sox. *Courtesy of W.J. Plott.*

On the night before their scheduled executions, Eula offered a last-minute confession that differed

WIFE'S "CONFESSION" FAILS TO PREVENT ELECTROCUTION OF THOMPSON AND JIM MOSS

FORMER BALL PLAYER PAYS DEATH PENALTY

James Moss, Once With Chicago Giants, Electrocuted In Georgia

WHITE MAN DIES TOO

Confession Of White Woman Fails At Eleventh Hour

Left, top: James Moss's execution in 1928 made headlines in the *Macon Telegraph*.

Left, bottom: James Moss headline in the *Baltimore Afro American*. *Author's collection.*

Opposite: Phrenology was a pseudoscience that claimed to reveal character traits by studying the shape of the head. *Public domain.*

from the story she told at court about a moonshine sale gone bad. Eula now claimed that she and a previously unknown lover killed Osbourne in order to frame her husband. Eula said that Jim Moss was an innocent hitchhiker who wasn't involved, having never met Moss before picking him up. Georgia Governor Hardman halted the executions to investigate, including inspecting photographs of the convicts' heads for phrenology clues. Governor Hardman, a physician, approved the executions, and Cliff Thompson and Jim Moss were led to the electric chair and executed on the same day, August 3, 1928.

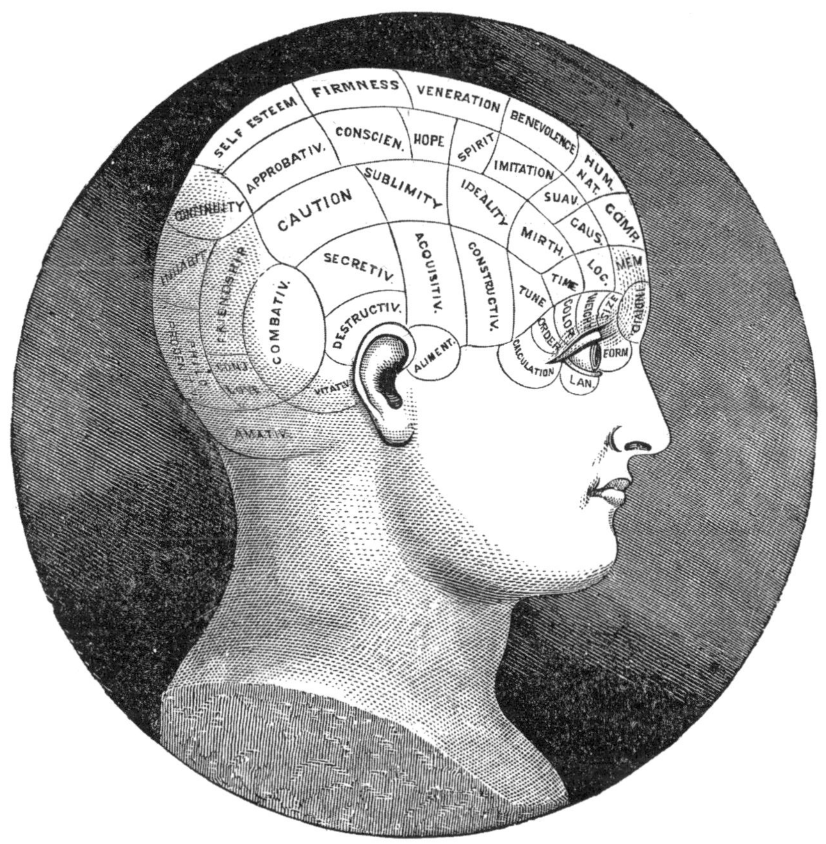

Next in line for the chair, Eula Thompson then offered another, even more convoluted story before her scheduled execution. This time, she implicated the now-deceased Moss. In this version, Moss was a crazed killer who murdered a store owner who shorted their change when they stopped for gas.

Eventually, Eula won over Georgia Governor Hardman, who commuted her death sentence to life, based in part on phrenology. She received parole, but in 1941, she was again convicted of murder for stabbing her brother to death, sending her back to prison. Eula Thompson again had her sentence commuted from death to life in prison, and she was paroled again and lived free until her passing.

DECATUR, ALABAMA

September 1922 found the Albany-Decatur Black Sox preparing for their Labor Day doubleheader with the Pulaski (Tennessee) Giants. Frank W. Johnson was managing the Black Sox, and southpaw Shotput Gamble was named the starting pitcher in game one for the A-D Black Sox, with another lefthander named Fields pitching game two. J.R. Martin, the team captain, probably wasn't worried, as Black Sox ace Shotput Gamble had racked up eighteen strikeouts against Pulaski on August 24. The teams met in several series at Albany's YMCA Park that summer, with a thirty-five-cent admission. Decatur also hosted games at Lakeside Park and Legion Field.

Decatur's Black Sox stepped up in 1926, hosting Montgomery's Grey Sox in a July series, followed by a visit from the Birmingham Red Sox and a team from Fayetteville.

Frank Johnson of Decatur is credited with organizing Morgan County baseball, arranging games, building the ballpark, promoting

The Brooklyn Royal Giants of 1916. *Back, from left to right*: Nat Strong, Doc Sykes, Max Rosner. *Middle, from left to right*: Andrew "String Bean" Williams, Charles Earle, Bill Kindle, Bill Handy, and John Pugh. *Front, from left to right*: Louis Santop, Pearl Webster, Ernest Gatewood, Joe Hewitt, and Lefty Harvey. *Author's collection.*

Doc Sykes, a Decatur native, threw a 1922 no-hitter for Baltimore and later was a crucial advocate for a fair trial for the Scottsboro Boys case. *Public domain.*

the team, managing the players, and bringing top-level opposition for exhibition games. The barnstorming Chicago Royal Giants played a series against Decatur in the spring of 1927. Johnson then purchased the Chicago franchise, and Decatur's club was known as the Decatur Royal Giants. They faced Chattanooga and Nashville at the team's new park, Cedar Lake, on Bee Line Highway. Otis Johnson took over as manager, and the club gained respect while facing the Black Barons and Chattanooga.

In 1928, the Columbia Cubs and Decatur Monarchs faced off at Decatur's Malone Park for a game expected to draw hundreds of fans. The following season, the Decatur Monarchs were guided by Joe Martin, who announced a lineup of Outlaw in center field, Kimball in left field, Benford in right field, Martin at third base, Sanders at second base, Jackson at shortstop, and McGinnis at first base. Boone was pitching the season opener to J. Martin behind the plate, with Draper in reserve and Reeves as a relief pitcher.

Labor Day was a popular date for big games. In 1929, the Decatur Monarchs took on the Birmingham Red Sox in a well-attended matchup at new Malone Park on Moulton Street.

No mention of Decatur's baseball history is complete without the inclusion of Doc Sykes, a top pitcher of the era as well as one of the most distinguished citizens in Alabama. In September 1922, Franklin "Doc" Sykes threw a no-hitter for the Baltimore Black Sox against the Atlantic City Bacharach Giants starter, Sam Streeter.

By 1926, Sykes had retired from baseball, was married, and ran a successful dentistry practice. Following the death of his father, Sykes moved his practice back to Decatur. In 1931, Doc Sykes was a leading figure in the city when he became an important advocate for equality during the trial of the Scottsboro Boys, refusing to be intimidated by Klan threats, abuse, and cross burnings at his home and office.

CHAPTER 8

1920s BIRMINGHAM'S BLACK BARONS

Bold Black Barons of the Jazz Age

Newspapers had called them "Bold Black Barons" and "Coal Black Barons," wordplay combining the name of Birmingham's white team with a description of the fans at West End Park, who often climbed dusty slag piles for free viewing of the games. The name caught on, and when Birmingham's entry into the Negro Southern League was organized, the moniker was officially adopted.

While the Black Barons debuted in 1920, the team was formed the summer before by Frank Perdue as "Perdue's Coal Black Barons." It's said that Perdue paid $200 for the Birmingham Stars club, but little documentation exists. Comprising top local players, the Black Barons were quickly on par with powerful industrial teams and sometimes dubbed the "All-Stars" for their talent-laden roster.

When the Negro Southern League launched, the Black Barons were charter members. Installing teams in large cities with spacious ballparks was part of Rube Foster and C.I. Taylor's plan for the NSL, and Birmingham's Rickwood Field was ideal. Represented by owner Frank Perdue at league meetings, Perdue was also elected president of the fledgling circuit. Birmingham's team was stocked with Industrial League talent—shortstop Buford "Geechie" Meredith and John Kemp from ACIPCO joined players from Ensley Steel Mill. Gordon Zeigler and Harry Salmon were also from local clubs.

Early view of Rickwood Field, with "colored" bleacher entrance on left and "whites" on right. *Author's collection.*

After dropping a road series and their May 3 home opener, they were chasing Montgomery and Knoxville in the standings. Perdue added players from the Cuban Giants team; Conrado "Red" Rodriguez was particularly effective, tossing multiple shutouts and long, extra-inning games. Another popular addition was Forrest "Wing" Maddox, the one-armed pitcher/outfielder who was reportedly batting .381 through July.

On August 21 at Montgomery, with the bases loaded and no outs in the inning, Black Barons infielder Jose Perez snared a sharp line drive near second base, catching it for the first out; he stepped on second base to double off the runner and tagged the approaching man from first for an unassisted triple play. Birmingham won, 3–1.

Rodriguez and Zeigler worked a double shutout on August 31, defeating Nashville in a doubleheader 6–0 and 9–0. In September, the Black Barons played a fifteen-inning tie in a game at Montgomery in which Birmingham's Juanelo Mirabal pitched brilliantly. Birmingham "won the game three times," but "the umpire robbed them at home plate" according to the *Birmingham News*.

Although the Black Barons finished in fourth place, the team drew massive crowds, including large numbers of white fans. Everyone seemed happy with the Black Barons' first season.

1921: Juanelo and the Two Jurans

Well, nearly everyone. A number of white residents living around Rickwood Field launched a protest to prevent Black teams from playing at the park. Newspapers noted that there had been no incidents, and the Rickwood contract was approved. The Black Barons were the top-drawing Black team in the South, and they were staying at Rickwood Field.

Perdue named himself manager, and Harry Salmon led the pitching staff, with Geechie Meredith handling second base. The season opened in front of more than five thousand fans, beating Montgomery's Grey Sox. Wing Maddox had two hits, including a triple. Steel Arm Dickey got the opening day start for Birmingham. After a first inning run, Dickey shut his former Grey Sox teammates out.

The rivalry between Birmingham and Montgomery was evident when early season games became heated. Both teams' second basemen were spiked, with "Big" Smith of Birmingham and "Tubby" Scales of Montgomery being ejected after scuffling with each other on the field.

On April 31, Juanelo tossed a one-hit shutout gem against the Red Sox at Memphis. Juanelo Mirabal was nearly always listed by his mononym Juanelo. The Tampa native of Cuban descent spent seven seasons with the Cuban Stars.

Steel Arm Dickey pitched a one-hit shutout of Knoxville at Rickwood Field on May 18. The portsider struck out eight, walked one, hit two batters, contributed a single, scored a run, and was hit by a pitch as the Black Barons

Rickwood Field, home of the Birmingham Black Barons. *Library of Congress, Prints & Photographs Division.*

Juanelo Mirabal was one of the Black Barons' ace pitchers. *Cuban card image courtesy of Mike Peich and Jim Creamer.*

won 7–0. On May 22, Dickey threw another gem, striking out fourteen in a victory at Mobile.

During a series in Mobile, officers arrested an umpire on the field when it was learned that the arbiter was betting on the game. Mobile fell that afternoon to Birmingham, 2–1. The Black Barons lost the final game, 5–4, in a contest that was reportedly laden with bad umpire decisions.

On July 26, 1921, John Juran became the first Birmingham Black Baron to throw a no-hitter, beating the Atlanta Black Crackers, 4–0, while striking out three in what was described as the "most thrilling game of the season" by the *Birmingham News*.

A pair of brothers on the Black Barons gave fits to journalists and newspaper typesetters. Often misspelled and confused in reports, Eli and John Juran (usually reported as "Duran" or "Durant") both pitched for Birmingham. Right-handed John "Bubba" Juran and left-handed Eli "Eagle" Juran were talented hurlers scouted from industrial teams.

The Black Barons started strong, especially at Rickwood Field, but scuffled midseason, dropping out of contention. Steel Arm Dickey jumped the team. Centerfielder "Big" Smith was injured and left fielder Holt broke a leg. The team shuffled its lineup to compensate but failed to jumpstart the club.

Birmingham's Holt led the NSL in batting average at .381. After spending most of the summer in third place, the Black Barons finished fourth in the standings.

1922: Birmingham's Soggy Season Cut Short

In February, C.I. Taylor passed away in Indiana following a bout of pneumonia. Rube Foster delivered his eulogy; Ben Taylor took over as manager of the ABCs.

At Black Barons' spring training, Geechie Meredith and Bob McCormack were among the returnees. Future Hall of Famer George "Mule" Suttles,

Robert Mitchell, and George McAllister were new to the club. Suttles was a five-time All-Star, two-time batting champion, and a triple crown winner in his stellar career. Credited with 179 home runs, George Suttles is second only to Turkey Stearnes. A Blocton, Alabama native, Suttles would be chosen to enter Cooperstown in 2006.

Birmingham dropped a hard-luck opener to start the season as Memphis edged them in extra innings. The contest was decided when first baseman George McAllister booted a groundball hit by the opposing pitcher. It didn't help that the Black Barons struck out twenty-two times that day. Birmingham lost the next six games and struggled for most of the summer. The highlights were few and rainouts abundant. Birmingham put together a winning streak around July 4, but the NSL fell apart. There was no formal announcement suspending play—it was simply a sudden lack of games.

1923: Black Barons Streak into the Big Time

The league reorganized, and Birmingham's Black Barons changed hands. Local hotel owner Joe Rush bought the team and was appointed league treasurer. Longtime catcher Poindexter Williams returned to manage, but only Geechie Meredith and pitcher Harry Salmon remained from the original club. George McAllister covered first base, and Mule Suttles, John Mitchell, and John Kemp were in the outfield; Bob Miller and "Two Sides" Wesley rounded out the lineup. Gordon Ziegler solidified the pitching staff.

Birmingham beat Memphis on opening day. John Juran's shutout set the pace for a successful season. The Black Barons simply destroyed NSL opponents. They knocked off New Orleans, Atlanta, Nashville, Memphis, and Pensacola, as well as won two of three games against the strong Twenty-Fourth Infantry Division of Fort Benning, who brought their sixty-piece band for support.

The streak began on May 18 when Birmingham played in the inaugural game at Memphis's new Lewis Park (later Martin Stadium). John Juran tossed a two-hit shutout to beat Memphis, 6–0. His brother, Eli, pitched the next day, allowing just three hits in another 6–0 shutout. Harry Salmon threw a shutout in game three, also allowing just three hits, winning 2–0.

The Knoxville Giants were then turned away scoreless during their two-game series. Atlanta was blanked twice at Ponce de Leon Park before scoring on a questionable balk call in an 11–1 loss to the Black Barons. That ended

BASEBALL TEAM (WON 33—LOST 6)

The Twenty-Fourth Infantry team of 1923 hosted an annual series against Birmingham's Black Barons. *New York Public Library.*

Birmingham's consecutive shutout streak at seven games in a row without allowing a run.

The Black Barons won twenty-two of their first twenty-four games, including pitching an incredible string of sixty-eight consecutive scoreless innings. No other team was able to win half of its games, while Birmingham boasted fifty-four wins and only six losses through mid-July.

Welcome to the Big Leagues

On July 15, Joe Rush purchased a league franchise, ushering the Black Barons into the Negro National League. Rush convinced Rube Foster that Birmingham could compete on the field and at the turnstiles, in spite of Birmingham's Sunday baseball ban. The Black Barons attracted more fans on weekdays than Foster's Chicago team drew for weekend dates. Rube conditionally acquiesced—Birmingham could remain as long as they continued to pull in large crowds.

The opponents now came from larger cities in the North; Milwaukee was the first to visit Rickwood Field in the major-league era of Black baseball in Birmingham. The *Chicago Defender* called it "a society event" in Birmingham as the teams battled to an epic 2–2 tie, finally called after twelve innings due to darkness. The following day, Friday, July 19, the Black Barons won their first game in the Negro National League, beating Milwaukee, 4–3, behind pitcher Harry Salmon. Birmingham's first major-league series netted two wins, one loss, and one tie.

The Black Barons kept pace in their first weeks at the top level. Fans were excited when Chicago arrived for a much-anticipated series. It was another society event with a jazz band providing music and many prominent citizens in the crowd. Circus seating was prepared in front of the bleachers for the overflow.

Harry Salmon worked brilliantly, scattering six Chicago hits in a shutout effort through six innings, nursing a one-run lead. As the sun was setting, the Giants' Charles Beckwith doubled and then scored to tie the game as umpires halted the contest due to darkness. For Birmingham, it was a tough series, as the Giants shut them out in game two and then beat them again in game three.

The pennant race was decided in August: Kansas City's Monarchs were season champs. Birmingham buzzed again for the Monarchs' first Rickwood visit. To boost the roster, Joe Rush acquired several new players. Bert Daniels, fresh from Army duty, pitched a two-hitter to beat the Monarchs. In game two, KC's future Hall of Famer Bullet Joe Rogan shut the Black Barons out easily.

BLACK BARONS ENTER NEGRO MAJOR LEAGUE

Rush Buys Reading Franchise; Milwaukee Plays First Game Here Thursday.

THE MAGIC CITY will have major loop was occasioned by the lack of

Birmingham's Black Barons joining the Negro Major League made headlines in the *Birmingham News*. *Author's collection.*

In the final game, the Monarchs ran wild, as they had the whole series, stealing eight bases. After the seventh inning, catcher Lewis Means "gave up in disgust" and was replaced. The Monarchs stole seventeen bases against the Birmingham backstop in three games, who caught just one thief in the series.

When the Giants returned to Rickwood, Harry Salmon battled Chicago's String Bean Williams but lost on three unearned runs. Birmingham let an early lead slip away in game two. Game three was Hall of Famer Cristobal Torriente's show, pitching a shutout and driving in all the runs with three hits, including a two-run homer over the Rickwood scoreboard as Chicago won 4–0.

The Negro National League was tough competition; Birmingham posted a record of fifteen wins against twenty-three losses.

1924: A June Swoon and the Unbreakable Slump

Sam Crawford was hired to manage, and the core of the Black Barons returned; Geechie Meredith, George McAllister, Mule Suttles, Poindexter Williams, and Harry Salmon were reliable stalwarts. Newcomers included Newt Joseph and Sam Streeter.

After opening the season in Memphis, Sam Streeter beat the Cuban Stars in front of more than ten thousand fans at the home opener. Birmingham won, but the talk in the Rickwood Field stands was about the sudden firing of manager Sam Crawford, who couldn't make it through one week before a disagreement with owner Joe Rush resulted in his termination. The Black Barons surged, sweeping the Cubans and then dispatching Candy Jim Taylor's Indianapolis ABC's at Rickwood, the Stars in St. Louis, and the Memphis Red Sox.

Birmingham was riding high in second place until a June road trip pitted them against powerful Chicago and league-leading Kansas City, bringing the streak of series wins to an abrupt close. The Monarchs swept them in Kansas City, prompting owner Joe Rush to acquire Dizzy Dismukes to manage.

The Black Barons responded by getting shut out by Chicago and then again in game two. Sam Streeter beat the Giants in game three at Schorling Park, but in the final game, the Giants held them scoreless again, allowing just one first-inning hit. Birmingham swept Detroit but then dropped three games in Cleveland. The road trip that began in second place ended with the club struggling to stay in contention.

The Black Barons started July facing the rival Monarchs, who hit eight homers and won three games as Birmingham's playoff hopes began to slip away. They then went to Chicago and lost. Detroit's Stars beat them, as did Memphis. Kansas City visited Rickwood again, sinking Birmingham out of contention for good. The slump included an eleven-inning loss to the Monarchs, a twelve-inning defeat by St. Louis on a bases-loaded walk, and Sam Streeter's no-hit bid broken up by a weak single with two outs in the ninth inning.

Hosting Atlanta in the final series of the season, the last contest was called off due to a lack of spectators. Birmingham finished sixth in the standings.

TWO BLACK BARONS ARE WORLD SERIES–BOUND

Pitcher Bill McCall was dealt to the Kansas City Monarchs during the summer, joining former Black Baron Newt Joseph, the Monarchs' third baseman. They would take part when the Monarchs faced Hilldale in the first "Colored World Series" in October 1924. McCall took a loss in game two, facing just three men in the first inning before being relieved. Montgomery-born Newt Joseph was more successful, hitting the first home run in Colored World Series history, an epic game that ended in a thirteen-inning tie. Kansas City won the ten-game series and the world championship.

Newt Joseph and Bill McCall, two former Black Barons, played in the first "Colored World Series," with the opening game taking place on October 11, 1924, in Kansas City, Missouri. *William A. Gladstone Collection, Library of Congress, Prints & Photographs Division.*

Mystery Plagues Black Barons No-Hit Feats

Willie Patterson was appointed as manager for 1925. His first act was to cut several stars from the roster. Two Sides Wesley, George McAllister, and John Juran were released in surprising moves. The team was a mixed bag with few returning players; longtime stalwart Geechie Meredith remained, as did pitchers Sam Streeter and Harry Salmon.

Birmingham opened against the Chicago Giants, who embarrassed them, 15–6, in front of more than eight thousand fans at Rickwood Field. The Giants swept them, and Birmingham struggled in the season's first weeks. After scuffling through a road trip to Indianapolis and Chicago, owner Joe Rush made a change, announcing a new manager. In May, Sam Crawford replaced Willie Patterson; Crawford and Rush had apparently made amends.

Never shy about making moves, owner Rush was often signing new talent and selling players to other clubs. However, trading pitcher Sam Streeter to Pittsburgh sent the team reeling. The Black Barons began a long tour of dates that often left them in the loss column.

Pitcher Robert Poindexter and battery-mate Poindexter Williams were two of the team's most reliable players. Catcher Poindexter Williams slugged a home run on June 8 that was reported as the longest hit in Detroit's Mack Park when the Black Barons downed the Detroit Stars, 8–6. Pitcher Robert Poindexter was one of the best in any rotation; on June 17, he shut out the Chicago Giants, allowing just two hits in one of his many sterling appearances.

On July 12, Black Barons starting pitcher Robert Poindexter pitched a no-hitter. Or perhaps it was a one-hitter. Or maybe two. Facing the Giants in Chicago, Poindexter allowed a groundball in the seventh inning that was misplayed, and it was reported to Birmingham papers as an error and to the *Chicago Defender* as a hit. Some other box scores published show two hits, but game reports reveal that the one questionable call was the only possible hit. Historians credit Poindexter with a no-no. Birmingham won 6–0.

A few weeks later, the Black Barons tossed their second no-hitter of the year, but like Poindexter's game, questions remain. Birmingham's pitcher was Willie Foster, Rube Foster's half-brother. Chicago owner Rube traded Willie to Birmingham, and Willie Foster responded by denying Detroit's Stars any hits on August 5, winning 5–0. The opposing pitcher was Turkey Stearnes, who allowed all five runs.

However, Willie Foster never played with the Black Barons again. Reportedly, Birmingham's third baseman, Stratton, was traded for Foster,

Poindexter Twirls No-Hit Game In Chi

CHICAGO, July 13.—Poindexter, of the Birmingham Black Barons, Sunday pitched a no-hit game here against the local team in the Negro National league. Poindexter was invincible throughout, while his mates fielded well behind him.

Score:		R.	H.	E.
Birmingham	000 020 210—	5	9	1
Chicago	000 000 000—	0	0	1

Poindexter and Williams; McColl. Padron, Miller and Brown.

BLACK BARONS BEAT STARS IN HITLESS GAME

Slagtown Crew Trades Stratton For Foster, Third Baseman

Top: Downtown Birmingham, circa 1925. *Author's collection.*

Bottom, left: Robert Poindexter's no-hitter made headlines in the *Birmingham News*. *Author's collection.*

Bottom, right: Willie Foster's Black Barons' no-hitter headline from the *Birmingham News*. *Author's collection.*

but three days later Stratton was back in the Birmingham lineup. Perhaps Rube regretted trading his half-sibling ace, or maybe the deal was a one-day loan to aid Chicago in the standings. It's also possible that Rube wasn't coherent. Just weeks earlier, Rube Foster had been found lying unconscious next to a leaky gas heater. Fume inhalation damaged his health, leading to erratic behavior, institutionalization, and early death. Why Rube traded his brother to Birmingham for one day may never be known, yet William Foster etched his name in the record books as a Black Baron.

Birmingham crawled out of last place, largely on the strength of Robert Poindexter's pitching. August was spent barnstorming, hosting the Houston Black Buffaloes (managed by Willie Patterson) and facing the Fort Benning team.

Birmingham was still a financial success. The *St. Louis Argus* estimated that the Black Barons brought in nearly $40,000 in two NNL seasons. However, travel expenses were a burden. Both Birmingham and Memphis canceled late-season road trips to save money. The Red Sox even chose five forfeits over travel.

CHAPTER 9

THE SATCHEL PAIGE ERA

1926: Black Barons Dominate in NSL Return

In January, it was announced that Birmingham's Black Barons had returned to the Negro Southern League. Joe Rush was elected league president. Control of the Black Barons then changed after a legal faceoff between Rush and Rube Foster. An unknown deal was struck behind closed doors, and Foster's league was left without Birmingham. The arrangement sent the Black Barons to the NSL under new stewardship, as Rush was forced to step down as owner in order to act as NSL president.

The new team president was Oscar Adams, editor of the *Birmingham Reporter*, a minister in the AME Zion Church, and graduate of Alabama A&M University, where he played trombone in an orchestra led by W.C. Handy. Adams's son Oscar Jr. was Alabama's first African American Supreme Court justice.

Clarence "Big" Smith was appointed manager, Geechie Meredith was back, George McAllister returned after a one-year absence, and catcher Poindexter Williams handled hurlers Harry Salmon and Eli Juran. Outfielders John Kemp and Joe Mitchell were re-signed.

Enter Satchel Paige

When the Black Barons' season opened in Chattanooga, on the mound opposing them was a lanky rookie pitcher later known the world over as Satchel. Leroy Paige beat the Black Barons, scattering just four hits.

The Rickwood Field home opener attracted a large crowd. Harry Salmon pitched the Black Barons to victory over Memphis, boosted by a home run from new outfielder Webb Oden. Following the game, Oden was sporting a brand-new Stetson hat, a reward from local businesses for opening day heroics.

The Black Barons were at ease back in the NSL, cruising into first place. Moundsmen Harry Salmon and Leo Burdine were excellent as the Black Barons knocked off Albany, Nashville, and Chattanooga. They swept the series against Fort Benning's Twenty-Fourth Infantry team and their band. A series loss at Memphis was the only bump in the road for the Black Barons, who returned to Rickwood Field on June 1.

Toeing the slab for Chattanooga was Satchel Paige, making his first appearance at Rickwood. Birmingham won the contest, 3–2, in eleven innings; Harry Salmon and Satchel Paige pitched all eleven. Two days later, Satchel played right field for Chattanooga, knocking two hits as the Black Barons won and swept the series.

Mobile's Leroy "Satchel" Paige was signed and sold to Chattanooga in 1926, setting him on a path to Cooperstown. *Los Angeles Times Photographic Collection, UCLA Library Digital Collections.*

Tearing through the opposition, Birmingham sealed its spot in the postseason and brought back Robert Poindexter to strengthen its already dominant starting rotation of Harry Salmon, Leo Burdine, and Charlie Beverly.

Satchel Paige returned with Chattanooga in August. Paige pitched nine innings, allowing five runs on ten hits and striking out five but losing as Leo Burdine shut out Chattanooga.

After being no-hit by Albany in July, Birmingham turned the tables on August 28. Harry Salmon threw his own no-hitter, winning 8–0 over Albany, striking out seven. Three days later, Robert Poindexter threw a one-hit shutout over Albany, adding two hits himself and scoring the only run of the game.

Memphis won the second half, setting up a playoff series that opened in Memphis. Two

The Albany (Georgia) Giants joined the Negro Southern League in 1926. *Dr. Layon Revel/ Negro Southern League Museum.*

Sides Wesley was managing the Red Sox. Harry Salmon pitched twelve innings, allowing just two runs, but Memphis starter "Steel Arm" Tyler also pitched twelve innings and allowed just two runs. The epic pitching duel ended in a tie due to darkness.

In game two, Geechie Meredith had a triple and double in a 9–4 Birmingham victory. Game three was a 1–0 nail-biter, won by Birmingham with just three hits against Memphis's emery-ball pitcher Bill Drake. The Black Barons came home to Rickwood Field with a two-game lead over Memphis. A special train ran between the cities for the popular series, which began with a rain-out.

The next day, Bill Drake opposed Robert Poindexter in a dramatic faceoff, battling scoreless through eight innings. In the bottom of the ninth with two out and the potential game-winning run at third base, Birmingham's manager approached the umpire. Clarence "Big" Smith challenged the pitches Drake had been throwing. Drake was a known emery-ball artist;

scuffing balls was illegal but rarely enforced, and he used the pitch openly. However, when the umpire was officially alerted that the ball had been scuffed, he was required to put a new one into play. Once he did, "Big" Smith, who was the next batter as well as the manager, drove the first pitch into centerfield as McAllister dashed home with the winning run.

With a three-game advantage, late runs led to a 2–2 tie in game five. In Memphis, the Black Barons won game six with Webb Oden's RBI single, 2–0. Memphis faced elimination.

Game seven was first rained out and then played to an eleven-inning scoreless tie as Bill Drake and Leo Burdine both pitched heroically. Refusing to quit, Memphis won games eight and nine, shutting Birmingham out on back-to-back days to force a final, winner-take-all game.

With the pennant at stake, Birmingham's Clarence "Big" Smith delivered three hits and scored four times to lead the Black Barons to the title. The final score was 9–3. Birmingham had won the Negro Southern League championship.

1927: Back to the Big Time

Birmingham would not defend its NSL championship; the Black Barons were back in the Negro National League. After their pennant-winning season, the announcement was met with great excitement. Reuben Jones was named manager, and many from the championship team returned, among them Geechie, Poindexter Williams, George McAllister, and pitchers Harry Salmon, Leo Burdine, and Sam Streeter. The Black Barons' spring training in Gadsden hosted more than thirty players vying for fifteen roster spots.

With ten thousand fans in the Rickwood stands, Birmingham opened the season against the Cuban Giants. Sam Streeter made the opening day start, tossing ten innings to earn the victory. Manager Reuben Jones got the new hat—his exciting tenth-inning, inside-the-park walk-off homer won the game and the annual Stetson prize.

Birmingham won the series, setting them on the fast track. A visit from Cleveland didn't faze them, winning four times and claiming first place. Then they hit the road…and the skids. By the time the Black Barons got back to Rickwood, they had dropped to third place and then fell to fourth after St. Louis arrived.

Sam Streeter faced the Red Sox in Memphis in June, allowing just one hit, but lost 1–0. Days later, Birmingham lost the game and three of their best players in one day. Pitcher Robert Poindexter was struck in the hand by a comebacker, catcher Poindexter Williams was injured by a foul ball, and Harry Salmon had to be carried from the field after sliding hard at home plate.

Ownership tried bolstering the lineup; a pair of players, including pitcher Columbus Vance, were poached from the Army team after the Black Barons dropped two games against the Twenty-Fourth Infantry but only played when they could get leave. However, another acquisition from that midseason spree would prove much more reliable. As Birmingham left for a twenty-game road trip, Leroy "Satchel" Paige was quietly acquired on June 17, earning $175 per month.

Welcome to the Black Barons, Satchel

One of the first mentions of Satchel Paige with the Black Barons is in a St. Louis game that ended oddly and was nearly tragic.

On June 27, Satchel dusted a batter off the plate and was then attacked by the hitter, Mitch Murray, who charged Satchel with a bat. Instead of fleeing, Satchel grabbed a bat and defended himself. Teammates restrained Murray and Paige, who were both ejected. Following the melee, a spectator jumped onto the field and tried to knife Geechie Meredith. The berserk fan was quickly mobbed by players and police, saving Geechie's life. Umpire Donaldson refused to allow Paige to continue pitching. Birmingham forfeited when the team refused to retake the field in protest of Paige's ejection. Two days later, Satchel Paige beat the St. Louis Stars as Geechie's grand slam lifted Birmingham to an 11–4 win.

Birmingham opened the second half of the season with a winning streak that sent them to the top of the standings, setting up an important homestand facing the Chicago Giants. The Giants' train arrived in Birmingham just fifteen minutes before game time; they stepped off the train and outscored the Black Barons, 9–7, to end the BBBs' eight-game win streak.

Birmingham lost the series but found momentum, picking up wins over Detroit and Nashville to put them back in first place. A series with second-place Kansas City went in the Black Barons' favor. In game three, Satchel Paige struck out eleven before being relieved in the seventh inning. Birmingham won the game and the series.

Satchel Paige first played on Mobile-area semipro teams with his brother, Wilson. *Los Angeles Times Photographic Collection, UCLA Library Digital Collections.*

Losses to Chicago and St. Louis sank them to third place in the tight NNL standings. While they were hosting a Labor Day tripleheader against Memphis, the Tuggle Band entertained the large Rickwood crowd. Game one ended in a 2–2 tie. In game two, Sam Streeter pitched the Black Barons to victory, allowing just three hits. Game three that day was a Satchel Paige seven-inning one-hit gem, pushing Birmingham into second place.

For the next day's doubleheader, Birmingham turned to Columbus Vance in game one. Vance beat Memphis, 2–1, allowing just one unearned run. Then Satchel Paige flirted with history, allowing one hit with two outs in the last inning of the nightcap in 9–0 win for his second one-hitter in two days. In just forty-eight hours, Birmingham played five games, winning four to jump from third place to first.

The final series matched Birmingham against the Cuban Stars. Harry Salmon won game one, and then Satchel struck out twelve, winning 5–0 as the Black Barons swept the Cubans and marched into the postseason to face the Chicago American Giants.

Rube Foster's Giants came to Rickwood and won two of three playoff games. The teams went to Chicago, where the Giants won twice more, ending the Black Barons' season.

1928: Satch's Black Barons

Restine Jackson, a real estate man, moved up from VP to team president and was elected to act as vice-president of the Negro National League. Jackson had played with Birmingham's Unions club in 1897 and remained close to the game. New manager Poindexter Williams brought back Geechie Meredith, George McAllister, Sam Streeter, and Harry Salmon. Also with the club were pitchers Satchel Paige, Robert Poindexter, and Leo Burdine, as well as infielder Dewitt Owens and outfielder Red Parnell.

St. Louis swept the opening series; one contest left Birmingham on the short side of a 20–2 drubbing. After being manhandled by Chicago, their record fell to one win in nine games. By the time Birmingham held its home opener, starting catcher/manager Poindexter Williams had a broken leg. Two Sides Wesley was brought in to manage as Birmingham had again changed skippers in the first weeks of the season.

More than seven thousand watched the Black Barons fall to Memphis in the home opener. Harry Salmon won the next day; Birmingham took the series by deploying their secret weapon. Satchel Paige relieved in the final game, striking out five of the ten hitters he faced and smacking two hits himself in the win.

Birmingham beat Cleveland five times in just three days, winning back-to-back doubleheaders at Rickwood. They found their next opponent, the Detroit Stars and slugger Turkey Stearnes, much tougher. Propelled by six Stearnes hits, the Stars won the series. Birmingham hovered around the .500 mark and was unable to put together much momentum.

On June 27, Robert Poindexter threw his second no-hitter against Chicago, winning 6–0 in seven innings. Poindexter's excellent season was highlighted by this pitching performance against his former team. The following year, 1929, Poindexter pitched a game with drastic consequences, playing so badly that even his Memphis teammates wondered if he "laid down." Later, his catcher tried to talk to the sullen pitcher, who would hear none of it. "Cheer up, big boy, today is ladies' day and you will probably go better with all the girls out there," said the catcher. "Boy, git away from me, I'm mad enough to shoot!" was the reply. Poindexter then pulled his pistol and fired one shot into the catcher's foot. The wounded man limped to the hospital, the pitcher was arrested, and Poindexter's baseball career was over. Catcher J.C. McCaskill's career was ruined as well, as his injury became infected and required an amputation.

Paige Rolling

Satchel Paige won the second game of a June doubleheader at Chicago, shutting out the Giants on two hits. A few days later, Satchel won again, striking out ten Monarchs in a 6–3 win.

Satchel kept rolling, making shorter starts and relief appearances between stellar pitching displays. Paige dazzled the St. Louis Stars, striking out nine and setting down the final fifteen hitters in a shutout. Satchel also knocked a pair of hits and scored once to boot. Paige occasionally played right field and even manned first base in a July game against St. Louis, rapping two hits in a losing effort.

Leroy Paige told reporters, "I don't mind you calling me Satchell [*sic*], but for goodness sakes, don't call me 'Big Boy'!" *Los Angeles Times Photographic Collection, UCLA Library Digital Collections.*

Satchel was back on August 14, beating Cleveland in thirteen innings. Paige came on in relief and allowed Cleveland to tie the game in the ninth. He then sat down thirteen batters in a row before the Black Barons finally scored the winning run. Satchel took a day's rest and then threw nine more innings, striking out seven to beat Cleveland again.

Birmingham then handled the Detroit Stars at Rickwood. Turkey Stearnes blasted two homers in the lone Detroit victory of the series.

A quirky set against Memphis wound down the season. One game took just sixty-seven minutes, and Birmingham won 3–0. Another ended when the Red Sox ran from a storm. Leading 3–1, Memphis tried stalling as the rain began, but Birmingham tied the score. With the bases loaded, torrential rain suddenly poured and the Memphis players raced for shelter as Leo Burdine trotted home uncontested, winning the game.

For Birmingham, it was an up-and-down season, relying heavily on Satchel Paige. The Black Barons led in attendance but finished fifth in the standings.

1929: Satchel Rules Rickwood

Two Sides Wesley returned to manage the Black Barons, who boasted a reliable core featuring Geechie Meredith, George McAllister, and pitchers Salmon, Burdine, and Satchel Paige.

After dropping their first series in Memphis, Rickwood's home opener welcomed the Cuban Stars. With ten thousand fans in the stands, Satchel Paige struck out seventeen hitters as Birmingham swept the series. Satchel again helped himself at the plate, smacking a two-run triple in game three.

Rickwood Field view from the pitcher's mound. *Library of Congress, Prints & Photographs Division.*

SATCHEL PAIGE ARRESTED FOR MURDER

Before spring training, Black Barons star pitcher Satchel Paige was in jail, facing possible murder charges. According to a report in Talladega's *Our Mountain Home*, on February 15 he shot Miss Elizabeth Ellis at her house in Talladega. Ellis died twelve days later. Paige was arrested for the shooting, according to reports in just two papers, Oscar Adams's the *Birmingham Reporter* and *Our Mountain Home*, which noted that he was "a pitcher for the Black Barons Baseball club."

Satchel told police that he didn't know the gun was loaded, playfully waving the pistol at her when it went off, accidentally shooting her in the neck. Satchel spent three weeks in jail before officials appear to have declared the shooting accidental, as no more information was made public. On March 2, the Black Barons covered Paige's Talladega expenses, including fifty dollars to a judge and nearly ninety dollars to a local doctor and hospital, which was later levied from Paige's salary. On April 13, the *Birmingham Reporter* ran the headline "Satchel Ready to Go," and no media mentioned the shooting again.

A few days later, Nashville fell victim to Satchel's dominance as Paige struck out eighteen batters and pitched all fourteen innings to win. The Black Barons played well over the first two weeks, but a series bashing by the Detroit Stars sent the club reeling. Lopsided scores convinced ownership that changes were needed. A flurry of moves brought back Clarence "Big" Smith, but still Birmingham scuffled.

Kansas City swept them, even beating Satchel 10–0 during a month-long road trip. Injuries continued to be a problem; catcher Poindexter Williams returned from his broken leg the previous season only to fracture a finger. Shortstop Ray Sheppard broke his leg on a squeeze play and was lost for the season. Then Poindexter Williams broke another finger.

If the Black Barons struggled in the standings, it wasn't the fault of Leroy "Satchel" Paige. The lanky right-hander was phenomenal, striking out fifteen Memphis batters in an eleven-inning June game. In July, he struck out seventeen Detroit hitters in a two-hit victory. During an August series in

Chicago, Sam Streeter tried to convince Satchel to jump to his Homestead Grays for more money, but Paige uncharacteristically refused. On the final day of the season, Satchel won the first game of the doubleheader and then came on in relief to win game two.

The Black Barons finished in fifth place but were easily the most popular team in Alabama.

1920s Baseball Across Alabama

In 1920, C.I. Taylor brought his Indianapolis ABCs to Birmingham for spring training and the organization of the NSL. The players, including stars Dizzy Dismukes and Oscar Charleston, were ensconced at the Hotel Dunbar.

Marion's Leonard Jones was badly injured when he broke his arm while delivering a pitch in 1920.

Anniston and Hobson City hosted a series between Red Circle and the Birmingham Black Barons in 1920.

The Gadsden Giants acquired Negro Southern League status in 1921 when the NSL expanded. The Giants, led by owner John Tyler, held games at League Park in Gadsden. Harvey Wacasey, Sig Mozey, and Buddy Meadows pitched for Gadsden, and Lottie Dale was the catcher for the club, which met opponents such as the Anniston Giants, the Rome (Georgia) Red Sox, and Attala (Alabama) teams. Gadsden hosted the St. Louis Giants in April for an exhibition series, losing twice.

Mobile's Braves and Bessemer's Stars were also added to the Negro Southern League in 1921; they would participate in the loop for one season before being replaced. Mobile's club defeated Bessemer, 5–4, on May 10, 1921; the *Birmingham Post-Herald* carried the score. Tally, Arnold, and Price were the battery for Mobile in the victory. Mobile would return to the NSL in 1923, often playing at League Park, built in 1918 and later called Hartwell Field. Mobile's white team's Monroe Park was destroyed by a 1926 hurricane, leading to improved facilities at Tennessee and Ann Streets.

In May 1921, a Rickwood series pitted the Black Barons against Mobile. Harry Salmon of Birmingham won game one; Mobile's pitcher Tally allowed twelve runs and got just two in support. Juanelo won game two, 7–5, in a contest that featured ten errors between the two teams. Game three also went to the Black Barons, who earned the series sweep with a shutout.

Admission was thirty-five cents to attend the Sheffield White Sox facing the Huntsville Tigers at the Madison County Fairgrounds in June 1921.

The Acton Black Devils were offering a challenge to any team "in their class" after knocking off the undefeated Montevallo club in 1921.

In September 1921, the St. Louis Stars opposed the Selma Blue Sox in a three-game series at Robbins Field on North Broad Street in Selma. Admission was thirty-five cents—a quarter for women. Selma was managed by E.B. Dent.

Birmingham's Garfield Park hosted Black baseball teams in the 1920s. Located on the south Bessemer line at Hilman station, the East Birmingham Cats and East Thomas All-Stars were among the clubs that faced off in the neighborhood ballpark.

The 1922 Tuskegee Institute club played under Coach Stagg's tutelage.

In June 1922, the *Anniston Star* reported that a game was being held in Anniston between the Red Circle Giants

Tuskegee baseball team, 1922. *Alabama Department of Archives and History.*

of Hobson City and Talladega's YMCA team "for the special benefit of the white community." The Red Circle Giants were a strong team that shifted its base a few times during its existence in the 1920s; they were also listed as hailing from Birmingham or Bessemer.

Tuscaloosa was brought into the Negro Southern League in 1922. Playing at Van Hoos Park, the team was led by John Price. Local newspapers suggested that they take on the name of the city's old team, the Black Warriors, but the club instead chose "Tuscaloosa Browns." The Browns hosted the touring Cuban Stars and several league teams during the '22 campaign. The following season, the team was called the Tuscaloosa Gray Sox. On July 4, infielders Robert White and Steve Harris completed a triple play against the Liberty Kaulton High Rollers; the game also featured a Rob White home run, and six Tuscaloosa players had triples.

In 1923, the Carrolton Black Giants took on a powerful Amory (Mississippi) team in a large July game. Reports from 1924 called the team the Carrolton Tigers, saying that the club was strong and well supported by fans.

The Marion Stars of 1923 shut out Selma, 1–0, in an exciting game that was attended by more than two hundred white fans, prompting Stars manager Robert Tubb to quickly have a grandstand built in order to accommodate spectators.

In 1924, the only excitement during the Fourth of July in Jasper, Alabama, was the ballgame between Jasper and "about five other teams" according to the *Daily Mountain Eagle*, which said that several prominent local citizens were on hand as spectators. The Jasper club had its own ballpark in town, hosting multiple games each week.

The Dothan team was playing at Pages Park in 1925, claiming ten wins against just one loss through the start of June.

In 1925, the West Point Tigers of West Point Alabama, were unbeaten in their ten games, the *Valley Daily Times* reported. "Had there been other games, Ike Chappel says they would have won them."

A report in the *Anniston Star* from August 9, 1925, mentioned the popular Oconee ball club of Boiling Springs taking on the Anniston Red Circle Giants in City Park at

Anniston. Boiling Springs, in Wilcox County near Camden, was a bustling location in the 1800s and sported a thriving farming community, but today the old village is practically a ghost town.

Kellerman's Tigers were facing the Uniontown Giants in 1925 in Northport as part of picnic festivities hosted by the Tuscaloosa County Fair.

A 1925 Dothan game featured two home runs, which delayed the contest when the balls couldn't be found; everyone waited while umpires sent someone to the hardware store to purchase a new baseball.

Montgomery's North Side Park on Lower Wetumpka Road was the site for games between the Western Railway team and the Atlanta Black Crackers in 1925, with Dismukes pitching the railway team to victory. The Western Railway team also faced the powerful McCoy-Nolan Giants barnstorming team that summer. The McCoy Giants would become the Milwaukee Bears and join the Negro National League the following year.

The dangers of being a field official were displayed in 1925 when umpire Joe Warrior was killed for making an unpopular call. Two neighborhood teams were facing off in Birmingham on June 24 when Warrior called a runner out at first base, causing a heated dispute and leading to the breakup of the game. As the umpire was leaving the field, he was accosted by one of the offended players armed with a large knife. As the arbiter tussled with the knife-wielding ballplayer, a woman approached and shot Warrior in the back. When the wounded umpire turned to face his shooter, the woman shot him again in the head, killing Joe Warrior instantly. At the sound of the shots, the large crowd dispersed in a panic just as the police arrived. In the fans' hectic crush to escape the grisly scene, one officer was struck by a car and suffered a broken leg. The assassin, Lizzie Perkins, was quickly arrested.

Selma hosted the Montgomery Grey Sox against Nashville in two games held at Robbins Field.

Luverne hosted Montgomery in 1926, playing on July 5. The two teams battled to a scoreless tie that was called after nine innings due to darkness in what was described as "an exciting ball game" by the *Luverne Journal* reporter.

Oneonta Park in Oneonta, Alabama, was hosting baseball in 1927 when the Attala ABCs opposed the Memphis Gray Sox there on May 27.

Ruckett's Stars were touted as one of the best teams in Scottsboro city history after they defeated Guntersville in a doubleheader, as reported in the *Progressive Age* on August 11, 1927.

Dothan's Giants were facing Albany (Georgia) in games held at Seminary Park on Range Street in 1927. South Range Street is currently home to Pitman Field, where baseball has been played continuously for more than sixty years. Games at Pitman in more recent decades include high school and Little League, and for twenty years the park hosted an annual Home Run Derby featuring major-league players from Alabama.

The Nebo (Alabama) girls' team defeated a team of Black girls from Oklahoma at White Sox Park in Cedar Lake in 1927, witnessed by a large crowd in a game promoted by Otis Johnson. Johnson's White Sox men's team also played a farcical game against the Nebo girls from Morgan County, winning 29–17.

The Cedar Lake White Sox, Decatur's rival team, under the control of promoter Otis Johnson, appointed Ross Malone manager. The club remodeled its park to seat two thousand

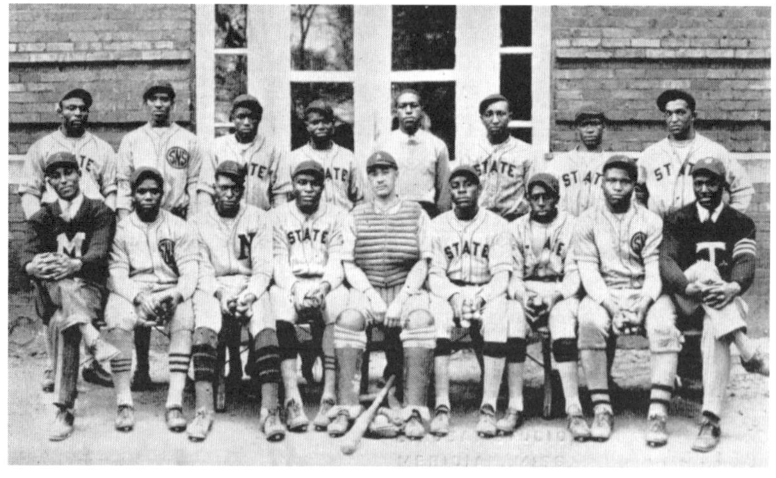

Alabama State University baseball team, 1929. *Alabama State University.*

and employed a full-time groundskeeper, Rip Adkins, ahead of its season opener with Hartselle.

In 1929, Tuscaloosa's Red Sox defeated Prattville, 4–2, in a close-fought game. Tuscaloosa's Red Sox would forge a long history in their city.

Anniston's Giants and the Opelika Blackbirds played lively games in 1929 at Fair Park, Anniston, continued fielding strong clubs and hosting touring and industrial teams.

The State Normal School baseball team often sent players to the Montgomery Grey Sox; the 1929 club featured four future Grey Sox.

1920s Black Baseball Is an Alabama Success

The 1920s saw baseball becoming big business, transforming into a national entertainment industry. Black entrepreneurs worked to build a better product on the field and innovated fan experience at the ballpark, while easily besting white teams in terms of fan support. National and international leaders in the sport recognized Alabama as a premier market and tapped into it often. Top teams made frequent visits to play in front of lucrative crowds. Birmingham and Montgomery were invited to join the prestigious new Negro Southern League. Montgomery's Grey Sox were successful on the field and at the turnstile, winning two league pennants. Birmingham's Black Barons quickly established the city as the premier city in the South for Black baseball and joined the top levels of the game.

Across Alabama, baseball fans enjoyed supporting talented teams in new ballparks hosting the best players in the sport. The old perils remained—racism, hard liquor, gambling, and wild living proved fatal to some. Yet many seized baseball's opportunity in Alabama, fueling bustling businesses and new entertainment ventures as well as cementing the state as a steppingstone to the top teams and major cities across the country.

CHAPTER 10

1930s MONTGOMERY

The Big Game: Satchel's Black Barons vs. Chicago Giants at Cramton Bowl

In August 1930, Montgomery fans packed Cramton Bowl for the biggest baseball event of the year: Satchel Paige and the Birmingham Black Barons taking on the Chicago American Giants behind their ace, Willie Foster. Already a crowd favorite, Satchel Paige pitched in the first game of the highly anticipated doubleheader.

Three thousand fans watched the Chicago Giants win both games. Fans marveled when Birmingham's Jimmy Crutchfield hit one of the longest homers in Cramton Bowl history in the first game, launching a shot to the deepest corner of the park in the seventh inning. The Black Barons' star hurler, Paige, took the mound in the seventh inning but was ineffective. Satchel surrendered six consecutive hits to Chicago, allowing four runs, but he did not factor in the decision.

There was a noticeable lack of coverage of Black baseball by the national press, including the Montgomery newspaper, around this time. That largely attended exhibition game featuring Satchel Paige and one State Teachers College versus Talladega rivalry contest are two rare mentions of Black baseball teams appearing in the *Montgomery Advertiser* during the 1930 season.

Cramton Bowl hosted many Negro League games. *Author's collection.*

1931: Grey Sox Make Comeback with New Park

The Montgomery Grey Sox opened the season with a grand parade through downtown Montgomery and a full program of entertainment with bands and vendors for the opening game against Birmingham at Montgomery's brand-new ballpark, located at the corner of Union and Thurman Streets (now University Drive North). Admission to new College Hill Park offered "popular prices" seating more than one thousand, with a special section in the grandstand for white patrons. Ladies Day was a popular Grey Sox promotion, often attracting hundreds of female fans taking advantage of free admission. The new park hosted a range of events from baseball to boxing to football. The white amateur city baseball league was invited to use the field for its games and accepted, holding many contests at the new Boguehome-adjacent ballpark. The Alabama State Hornets baseball and football teams played there for decades and continue to use the stadium for athletics.

Some Grey Sox games were at Cramton Bowl when bigger crowds were expected. In June, the first night game between Black teams was held under the lights at Cramton Bowl as the Grey Sox defeated Birmingham.

Both Marion Cunningham and Henry Hannon spent time managing. Cunningham moved to first base as a player/manager, with brother Herman

Above: Montgomery Stadium entrance, circa 1937. *Alabama State University.*

Left: Catcher Paul Hardy, shown with the Chicago American Giants, also played with Birmingham, Montgomery, and others. *Memphis and Shelby County Room, Memphis Public Libraries.*

Cunningham taking over at shortstop. The Grey Sox lineup cards were filled with a long litany of names this season, often with last name only. The opening day announcement gave the starting rotation as simply "Lockhart, Nelson, Peterson and Turner." Although newspapers downplayed the Grey Sox players, the 1931 Montgomery roster featured some excellent talent, including a stellar rookie catcher named Paul Hardy.

Born in Mississippi in 1910, Paul Hardy would have a long career as a player and manager with some of the best teams in the Negro Leagues, particularly the Memphis Red Sox. After his playing days, Hardy logged millions of travel miles as the bus driver for Abe Saperstein's Harlem Globetrotters. With Montgomery, Paul Hardy built a reputation for durability, catching both games of doubleheaders eleven times for the Grey Sox, and provided a solid bat in the lineup.

Also on the Montgomery roster were two other rookies, Felix Manning and Johnny Ray. In his final season, Johnny Ray mentored Jackie Robinson with the KC Monarchs. Felix Manning would be the longtime manager of the Atlanta Black Crackers.

G-Sox Regulars Include Prof, Wingfield, High Pockets, and Ace

Montgomery's "Lockhart" was George H. "Prof" Lockhart, a coach and teacher with the State Teachers College from 1926 through the 1960s. An outstanding pitcher by the time he appeared for the Montgomery Grey Sox, thirty-year-old Lockhart had already played with the Bacharach Giants and the Chicago Giants.

George H. "Prof" Lockhart. *Alabama State University.*

Prof Lockhart's Alabama State Teachers College basketball teams won seven state championships in the 1940s. In 1932, Lockhart coached the Alabama State football team to a 9-0 record and handled the school's esteemed baseball program for decades. ASU has a building dedicated to honor George Lockhart. Prof Lockhart was selected for the AHSAA Hall of Fame in 2003.

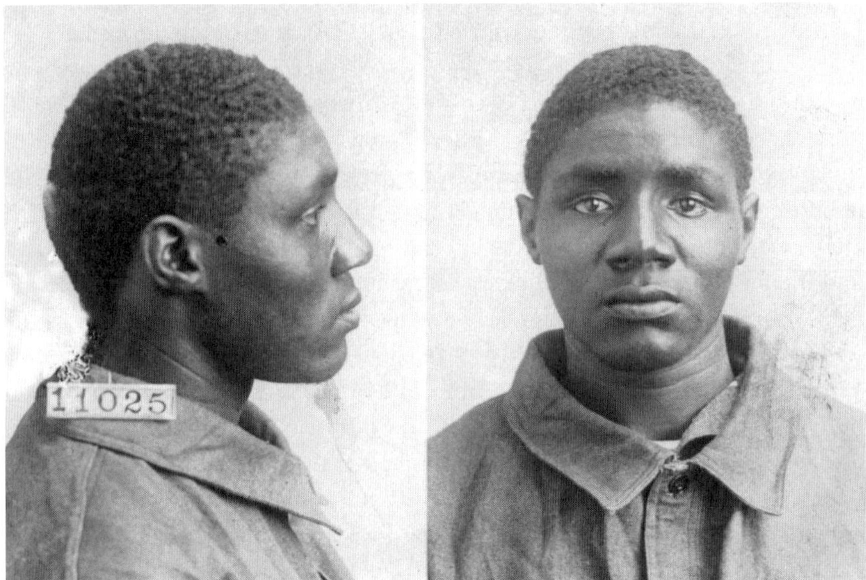

David Wingfield's mug shot from Leavenworth Prison. *Public domain.*

The Grey Sox's David Wingfield, a slick-fielding second baseman, was a veteran of the Negro National League as well as the highly competitive Leavenworth Federal Penitentiary Baseball League. One of the "Booker T Four," Wingfield was among four players from the Leavenworth league's only Black team called the Booker Ts. The Booker T Four would all go on to play pro baseball following their releases. The Booker Ts were one of the top teams in the region, facing premier clubs such as the KC Monarchs.

As a member of the Tenth Cavalry "Buffalo Soldiers" Regiment, Wingfield served time for the shooting death of a fellow soldier in 1915. Dave Wingfield returned to baseball upon gaining his release from military incarceration, popping up for just a few games during the 1920s with teams in Detroit, Washington, and Dayton.

In 1931, he came to Alabama after a year spent serving time on a Georgia chain gang and signed with Montgomery's Grey Sox. Nearly forty years of age, Wingfield played just one season in Montgomery before disappearing to time after the Grey Sox last games' final outs were recorded.

The pitcher humbly listed as "Turner" is Tom "High Pockets" Turner, who would attend Alabama State Teachers College/ASU in '34 under a sports scholarship. From 1936 to 1939, "High Pockets" Turner played for the Dayton Marcos and Cincinnati Braves, the only Black teams in the otherwise all-white semipro Indiana/Ohio League. During World War II, Turner captained the Army's Ninth Service Command Unit baseball team, which swept the 1942 Military World Series. After the war, Turner played for the Chicago Giants and in Mexico before managing his local Valley Giants in Ohio. Active in the civil rights movement, Tom joined Dr. King for the March on Washington in 1963 and two years later was among those marching with Dr. King from Selma to Montgomery. Tom "High Pockets" Turner died peacefully at the age of ninety-seven in Georgetown, Ohio.

Pitcher Peterson was rookie Harvey Peterson, getting his first taste of pro ball with Montgomery as a second baseman and relief pitcher. Peterson, a Selma native, went on to pitch for several clubs, including Birmingham, Knoxville, Memphis, Cleveland, and Cincinnati.

The pitcher Nelson was Everett "Ace" Nelson. He played two seasons with Montgomery before pitching for the Indianapolis ABCs. Nelson was noted for pitching extremely well with the Grey Sox.

Grey Sox Publicity Stunt Gets Hairy

The Montgomery Grey Sox created a stir when word got out that they had scheduled dates with the House of David. The famous bewhiskered barnstorming ball team from Benton Harbor, Michigan, had a reputation for being open to play Black teams. For Montgomery city leaders, the concept of a team of white men facing a team of Black players on a local diamond was completely unacceptable, no matter the circumstances.

Just as some narrow-minded locals were beginning to think of wielding pitchforks and lighting torches, a follow-up in the *Montgomery Advertiser* titled "No Need for Concern, Mr. Jim Crow!" informed the public that the House of David team in question was the Cuban House of David, comprising mostly African Americans and Cubans. Organized by promoter Syd Pollack, the club had recently begun introducing "shadowball" routines to audiences.

The Cuban House of David featured slugger Charlie Mason (from Montevallo, Alabama) and many African American players. Its main Cuban connection was legendary Cuban pitching star Luis Tiant, father of former Boston Red Sox All-Star Luis Jr. The Grey Sox defeated the Cuban House of David, scoring four ninth-inning runs in an exciting walk-off victory at College Hill Park, reportedly the only defeat the Cuban team suffered during

Cuban House of David, 1931 advertisement. *Author's collection.*

their southern tour. A few weeks later, they returned, pounding Montgomery in a doubleheader by scores of 20–1 and 9–7.

While the furor over the House of David visit was brewing, the Grey Sox hosted the Cleveland Cubs for two games. The legendary Satchel Paige and former Grey Sox hurler Sam Streeter were the top moundsmen for the Cleveland Cubs, who edged the Grey Sox behind Streeter, 4–0, in front of a good crowd.

As a publicity stunt, the House of David promotion was wildly successful. The games were well attended; the team received a great deal of attention from the press and left some outspoken segregationists red-faced. However, while the team did force its way back into the newspaper, the initial reaction to the possibility of mixed-race baseball clearly revealed some residents' true feelings.

Montgomery Shares Mysterious 1931 Championship

While the Grey Sox struggled in the first half of the season, coming in fifth with a 14-22 record, Montgomery surged to win the second half and earn a postseason spot. However, with the league championship series against the Memphis Red Sox tied at three games apiece, the last game was never played for reasons unknown. Montgomery and Memphis were NSL co-champions for 1931.

A NO-HIT WIN FOR THE GREY SOX

Facing the Memphis Red Sox in a doubleheader on May 30, the Grey Sox defeated Memphis in the second game without the benefit of a single hit. In the nightcap of the doubleheader, a third-inning Memphis error led to an unearned run for the Grey Sox, which stood as the difference in the game. Montgomery's pitcher Ace Nelson allowed just three hits, shutting out the Red Sox.

1932 Big-League Montgomery

Due to the collapse of the Negro National League, the Negro Southern League became a de facto major league, giving Montgomery big-league status for 1932. The NSL teams were well covered across the country, although many important details are still unknown. Fans from across the South turned out in large numbers to watch the Grey Sox. The games were so popular that Western Railway offered special baseball travel packages for fans in other cities who wanted to attend Grey Sox games. More than one thousand attended Cramton Bowl on August 1 to see Montgomery defeat Atlanta, 7–1; many paid one dollar for round-trip tickets from Georgia.

Frank Lewis with the Alabama State baseball team. *Alabama State University.*

Henry Hannon Jr. managed the team and was the man filling out Montgomery's major-league lineup cards. The Sox roster was largely composed of newcomers, mixing younger players with veterans, many with college experience and many possessing classic nicknames.

On the Grey Sox infield, Matt "Lick" Carlisle was deployed at shortstop. Keystone duties were handled by Montgomery native Oran "Duck" Frazier and backup second baseman "Dusty" Decker. Veteran James "Curly" Gurley took over at first base after Felix Manning suffered an injured leg in June. Newcomer Matt Jackson played third base, with soft-handed Paul Hardy again wearing the tools of ignorance behind the plate for most Grey Sox games. In the outfield, Frank Ray, "Joe Mitchell," and Frank Lewis were patrolling the grassy knolls of College Hill Park.

The major-league Grey Sox pitching rotation was led by Lefty Calhoun, along with Everett "Ace" Nelson and George Mitchell doing most of the pitching for Montgomery. Prof Lockhart also helped with good mound work, including defeating the Cuban Stars in an April game.

Lick, Dusty, Ace, and Bearcat

Matthew "Lick" Carlisle with the Homestead Grays. *Robert H. McNeill Family Collection, Library of Congress, Prints & Photographs Division.*

Matthew "Lick" Carlisle was born in 1910 in Wenonah, Alabama's coal fields, where he worked in the mines before playing for the Birmingham Black Barons in 1931. When Lick joined the Grey Sox, the speedy infielder was a rising star. Carlisle would go on to play with the Memphis Red Sox and Birmingham Black Barons before settling in at the top of the batting order for the powerful Homestead Grays. Matt Carlisle later served in the U.S. Navy during World War II and then returned briefly to baseball as a utility infielder.

Charles "Dusty" Decker was born in Kentucky and grew up in Indiana. Decker attended Fisk University and then Lincoln University, where he earned honors as quarterback of the football team as well as the nickname "the Human Cannonball" for his gridiron play. By 1931, Dusty Decker had signed with the Indianapolis ABCs under Candy Jim Taylor's watchful eye. In '32, Decker arrived to fill Montgomery's shortstop position, which he handled capably.

Everett Nelson, aptly dubbed "Ace" Nelson, pitched well for the Grey Sox, losing just once and logging five complete games as Montgomery's top starting pitcher. Ace Nelson also helped out with a few innings in the outfield and even took a turn at second base. The following season, the right-hander toiled for the Indianapolis ABCs.

Walter "Bearcat" Calhoun pitched and played occasional outfield for Montgomery. The young hurler would have a long career pitching for a variety of teams, including the Indianapolis ABCs and St. Louis Stars, where he was known as "Lefty" Calhoun.

Montgomery's Three Mitchells

Or four. Or maybe five. One player on the Grey Sox was often listed as pitcher "C. Mitchell," likely a typographical error, as several players named Mitchell appear with Montgomery, yet none of them had the first initial of "C." Also, the outfielder "Joe Mitchell" is a mystery, as there was no Joe among the Mitchells who play for the Grey Sox in 1932. There is a Joe Mitchell, but he was not on this team. All of the Grey Sox Mitchells played a little right field, but none was a regular outfielder and two were pitchers. It is unknown how, or if, any of the Mitchells were related.

George Mitchell in 1924 from the *St. Louis Argus*. *Public domain.*

Grey Sox hurler George "Big" Mitchell was in the middle of a thirteen-year career. A veteran moundsman, George had already pitched with the Chicago, Indianapolis, Kansas City, and St. Louis. George Mitchell got the opportunity to sign with the Grey Sox when the Negro National League folded, leaving many players looking for work. Later, the well-respected Mitchell was chosen to manage in the All-Star Game at Chicago. For Montgomery, George Mitchell pitched and played some right field.

The Grey Sox John Mitchell is not to be confused with John Mitchell Sr., the Autauga Country native who much later played with the Detroit Stars. Montgomery's Johnny Mitchell appeared as backup catcher and spent a few innings in right field.

Also with Montgomery was pitcher Alonzo "Hooks" Mitchell, called "Fluke" for his sweeping sidearm curveball and his bowed legs. Alonzo would later pitch for and manage the Jacksonville Red Caps. A veteran right-hander who could also play a little first base and handle occasional outfield chores, Mitchell had previously been with the Bacharach Giants and Baltimore Black Sox.

Montgomery's Three Fraziers

Albert Frazier was learning second base, just sixteen years old from Jacksonville, Florida. Frazier would go on to become the head football coach of Savannah State University. Albert Frazier, born in 1915, was the youngest Grey Sox major-league player and the last one to pass away, dying in 1999. Albert is not to be confused with Montgomery-born Oran "Duck" Frazier, also a second baseman for the Grey Sox. Oran had been a star at Alabama State Teachers College, where he was captain of the football team as well as second baseman for the Hornets baseball team. Later, he would be principal of a school in Evergreen, Alabama, where he lived until his death in 1992. Oran was the brother of Severn Frazier, who also appeared with the Montgomery Grey Sox this spring. Severn had been an athletic star alongside his brother at Alabama State University.

Chaser, Curley, and Tremble

Felix "Chaser" Manning shared time at first base for the Grey Sox. Manning, a right-hander who made occasional relief pitching appearances, was from the Birmingham area, where he starred in the Industrial League. Later he would manage in Atlanta.

Left-handed pitcher Clarence "Red" White had appeared with teams such as Memphis, Nashville, and Louisville.

James Gurley was a popular pitcher for many teams, including the Memphis Red Sox and the Chicago Giants. For Montgomery, "Curly" Gurley split time between pitching and the field. He was capable in the outfield and first base.

Others on the Montgomery roster have more elusive histories. James (sometimes Joe) "Steel Arm" Bell was a catcher and outfielder as well as occasionally pitcher, but little more is known of his career until 1940, when he appeared briefly with Indianapolis. He may also have played with Birmingham. This is not the famous "Cool Papa" of the Pittsburgh Crawfords, but he might have been the saxophonist with the Black Birds of Paradise.

Frank "Tremble" Trimble appeared at second base and later barnstormed with the St. Louis Blues. His Grey Sox appearances may have caused collegiate ineligibility.

Frank Lewis. *Alabama State University.*

James Pope had appeared with Louisville the previous year; after this season, little more is known about him.

Walter Goines was credited with pitching a few times and getting into the outfield once for the Grey Sox before he disappeared from baseball.

A. Matthew Jackson was solid at third base and occasionally at shortstop for Montgomery. In his twenty-six official games with the Gray Sox in '32, Jackson was credited with twenty-nine hits, seventeen runs batted in and a .290 batting average. Other than three seasons with the Grey Sox and brief action split between Birmingham and Cincinnati, little is known about Matt Jackson, who logged the highest WAR (wins above replacement) among hitters in Montgomery's only major-league season.

Frank Lewis paced the Grey Sox with his .303 batting average, striking out just one time in twenty-two major-league games while wearing a Montgomery uniform. Besides his statistics for the Grey Sox, little is currently known about Frank Lewis, an ASU shortstop.

Outfielder Frank Ray had attended Morris Brown University. The Georgia native died in Tuskegee in 1963.

Grey Sox Major-League Games

Montgomery opened its major-league season on April 23, defeating Atlanta's Black Crackers in a thrilling victory as the G-Sox held Atlanta to four hits on opening day at the newly refurbished College Hill Park. Atlanta scored first in the top of the fourth inning; the Grey Sox answered in the bottom of the inning with a run of their own, the first in Montgomery's major-league season. Montgomery added two runs in the sixth and one in the eighth inning to seal the 4–1 victory. Hardway and White were the battery for the Grey Sox.

The Grey Sox came back the next day and won twice, shutting the Crackers out in both ends of a doubleheader to sweep their first major-league series. A few weeks later, the Grey Sox defeated the Atlanta Black Crackers, 11–1, at Ponce de Leon Park as part of the opening series there.

MONTGOMERY'S MAJOR-LEAGUE RECORD IN QUESTION

As a major-league team, the Grey Sox's official win-loss record is a gray area. Most reliable baseball sources show the Montgomery Grey Sox in fourth place overall for the 1932 Negro Southern League standings, but few agree on the details. In their lone season as a major-league team, the Montgomery Grey Sox are sometimes credited with twenty-three wins against twenty-five losses with one tie. Or sometimes twenty-eight wins and eighteen losses. Montgomery's true win-loss record is an evolving project for baseball historians, as researchers work to recover and tabulate the information of the Negro Leagues.

Negro Southern League results were riddled with technical mistakes, typos, faulty mathematics, and loose reporting standards. As a result, Montgomery is yet to be able to "officially" herald its first major-league winning pitcher, to credit its first victorious major-league lineup, or to celebrate the anniversary of the most historic event in the city's long baseball history: the Grey Sox's first major-league win. Regardless of the details, Henry Hannon Jr. was the first manager from Montgomery, Alabama, to win a major-league baseball game and did so as skipper of his own Grey Sox. It is an honor befitting the man so important to Montgomery's baseball history.

Alabama State University baseball park's entrance was major league in 1932. *Author's photo, 2025.*

Location of Alabama State University's original baseball field, home of the Montgomery Grey Sox. *Author's photo, 2025.*

Montgomery dropped the other three games and only won one of four in Birmingham as the Grey Sox began to struggle following the opening month of the season.

During Montgomery's big-league season, the team faced many tough opponents. One of the first challenges was the Cuban House of David. The Grey Sox erupted with a late rally to defeat the Cubans in the ninth inning.

In June, Montgomery plated four runs in the ninth inning against Little Rock in the first game of a doubleheader. Then Montgomery's "Steel Arm" Bell tossed a shutout in game two as part of a series sweep as Paul Hardy caught both games.

The Grey Sox often scored ten or more runs in a game. In April, they defeated a team from Carolina, 13–3, rapping seventeen hits. The following day, the two teams each tossed a shutout to split a doubleheader, displaying their pitching prowess. In May, the Grey Sox trounced Atlanta, 11–1, in a league game.

The team was forced to postpone a July game in Knoxville when their car broke down near Atlanta. The club continued the season without any further schedule interruptions until September, when it was suddenly reported that the Grey Sox had disbanded.

CHAPTER 11

BIRMINGHAM'S BARNSTORMING BLACK BARONS

1930 BBBs Start Strong

The Black Barons had a lot of new faces, either freshly acquired or with less than a season in Birmingham. Several players, such as Geechie Meredith, were lured to other teams before manager Clarence "Big" Smith's team opened camp at Fort Benning. A new infield took shape with David Thomas at first and Otto Mitchell replacing Geechie at second. On the left side of the infield, Elmer Carter played shortstop, and Claude Johnson handled the hot corner. The outfield consisted of Burnsville, Alabama's Herman "Jabbo" Andrews, Mobile native Terris McDuffie, and Jimmie Crutchfield. Catcher William Perkins was a reliable receiver for the pitching staff, led by Harry Salmon and lefty Columbus Vance. Southpaw Sam Streeter was lured back, but Satchel Paige went to Baltimore.

Herman "Jabbo" Andrews, a native of Burnsville in Dallas County, won the 1933 NNL batting title. *Dr. Layton Revel/ Negro Southern League Museum.*

The Black Barons opened their schedule at home against the Cuban Stars in front of more than eight thousand spectators, winning 4–1 for Harry Salmon, who struck out eight. Birmingham lost just once in the series. The Black Barons came home after two road series in first place. Hosting Nashville, Birmingham swept the series as fans began to take note of the hot start and new talent on the squad.

A trip to St. Louis and Kansas City put a stop to the hot start, as Birmingham dropped three games in each city and was hit hard. Ownership, led by Restine Jackson, made midseason moves to improve the club; infielder Dewitt Owens and pitcher Satchel Paige were wisely brought back.

The Black Barons went back on the road as the team looked to right the ship. However, they lost three of five games against the Detroit Stars, learning during the series that former teammate Robert Poindexter had been killed, casting a gloom over the clubhouse.

Facing Memphis's Red Sox at home, Birmingham foolishly traded Jabbo Andrews, shortstop James West, and ace pitcher Harry Salmon to Memphis during the series. Memphis, with several former Black Barons already on their roster, beat Birmingham easily. Harry Salmon pitched twice for Memphis, striking out many of his ex-teammates and winning game four.

As the first half closed, Birmingham was last in the standings but near the top of the league in attendance.

Satch Is Back

Satchel rejoined the Black Barons with a twelve-strikeout effort against Detroit in mid-July; however, the Detroit Stars took the series. Against St. Louis, Satchel again provided the only victory of the series.

Bill Gatewood was brought in to replace "Big" Smith as manager. It was a popular move, as fans were frustrated watching Birmingham scuffle when anyone not named Satchel Paige was on the mound. With the Black Barons, Satchel was simply outstanding, piling up strikeouts and hurling the sphere with legendary efficiency in nearly every outing. In July, Paige tossed a four-hit shutout with ten strikeouts. In August, he punched out twelve Chattanooga hitters to win, and a start against Chicago earned him ten more Ks.

A series against the Chicago Giants loomed large, but the Black Barons erupted to win the set when Streeter won a pair of games. The club set out on a four-city tour, making stops in St. Louis, Chicago, Detroit, and Nashville. While on the road, Satchel was again involved in an on-field melee; in Chicago, the Giants' bat-wielding Eddie Miller chased him across the field.

Left: With Birmingham, Satchel Paige led the league in strikeouts in 1928 and 1929. *Los Angeles Times Photographic Collection, UCLA Library Digital Collections.*

Opposite: Geechie Meredith and Saul Davis, with the 1925 Black Barons. *Image courtesy of W.J. Plott.*

Birmingham was swept in Detroit and then struggled in Nashville and never seemed to find its stride. Coming home for a Labor Day doubleheader, the Black Barons' Sam Streeter won game one. Satchel Paige then allowed just three hits to win the second game, striking out three in his final outing in a Birmingham Black Barons uniform (for the moment).

Satchel was excellent for Birmingham, especially at home. Paige took the hill for eight games at Rickwood, starting six games, pitching twice in relief, and winning six times.

1931: Return to the NSL Brings Shadowball

Rube Foster died in December 1930, leaving Black baseball without its longtime leader. After years of complaints from other NNL teams about travel, the southern clubs were sent back to the Negro Southern League. The NSL, announced as an eight-team loop, only listed six clubs in the standings. Charles Johnson represented the Black Barons at the league meetings; Birmingham's Restine Jackson was elected league president. Frank Perdue was reported as owning the team again, likely backed by an unknown investor.

Geechie Meredith was signed to manage the Black Barons. Pitchers Harry Salmon, Columbus Vance, and Leo Berdine returned. Also back were outfielders Terris McDuffie and Jabbo Andrews, catcher Bill Perkins, and infielder Willie Carter. George McAllister also returned, and the team added "Lick" Carlisle and pitcher Bob Veale.

An exhibition series against the Cuban House of David introduced fans at Rickwood Field to a legendary act in Black baseball. Birmingham won the first game but then lost three to the Cuban team, who dazzled the huge Rickwood crowds with brilliant "shadowball" pantomime acts.

Fans were barely in their Rickwood Field seats for the home opener against Chattanooga when Black Barons shortstop Pee-Wee Cooper was hit by a pitch, knocking him unconscious. Cooper shook it off and stayed in the game. Birmingham won on Harry Salmon's pitching and Leo Berdine's three hits. A trip to Memphis added two more wins to Birmingham's ledger.

When they returned for the next Rickwood series against the Red Sox, Birmingham had traded Pee-Wee Cooper and bought a catcher from the House of David. Memphis was unimpressed, winning the three-game set. The two teams then traveled to Little Rock, where Memphis again swept them. In mid-June, the Black Barons were in fourth place, hovering around the .500 mark.

The Black Barons climbed to third place, winning about as often as they lost. After Independence Day, the schedule was always heavy with exhibitions and barnstorming dates. Walter Calhoun threw a no-hitter against Fort Benning in the annual contest against the Army team, but it was all downhill after that. Birmingham struggled at Rickwood, mercifully losing some games to rain. In August, the Cuban House of David returned to win a night series at Fair Park.

When Pensacola couldn't make an August series appointment in Montgomery, the Black Barons filled in, falling to the Grey Sox.

NIGHT GAMES

Night baseball was gaining popularity, and evening start times began to appear on schedules. On June 17, the Black Barons faced the Grey Sox at Montgomery's Cramton Bowl in the first night game between Black teams at the ballpark on Madison Avenue. Montgomery won 3–1 under the lights.

On July 6–7, the Black Barons and Red Sox were in Birmingham, but not at Rickwood. Fair Park field was the host, as new lights illuminated two night games. Birmingham's Harry Salmon pitched well, allowing just five hits to earn the win. On the second night, Geechie hit a home run to propel his club to another victory.

When Knoxville was unable to fulfill their Montgomery dates, Birmingham again stepped in and again dropped the series. They then barnstormed the Midwest against a variety of teams with sparse reporting. The Black Barons limped back to Birmingham, playing unpromoted games against Industrial League teams to finish the year quietly. NSL final standings, if produced, were not publicized.

1932: Stormy Weather

The Depression idled Black major leagues, leaving the Negro Southern League as the top circuit. NSL reorganization included some northern teams, but the loop again had a tenuous grip on its business.

In January, tragedy struck the Black Barons when manager Geechie Meredith was killed in a mining accident. Meredith, who worked in the mines before and during his career, was electrocuted by an exposed wire at his Sayreton mine workplace. He was thirty-two years old.

Catcher Poindexter Williams was signed to replace Geechie as manager. George McAllister returned, as did Harry Salmon. Others included James West, Harry "Spoon" Carter, and Alonzo Boone.

Opening in Memphis, the Black Barons split the series after an opening night 7–3 win. The Birmingham home opener at Rickwood brought the Pittsburgh Crawfords, who swept them.

A pair of wins over Louisville offered hope, quickly dashed at the next stop in Chicago. Chicago's Giants, under new leadership after Rube Foster's death, ruthlessly hammered the Black Barons, sweeping three games while scoring twenty-six runs. Ownership made moves; George McAllister replaced Poindexter Williams as manager. The Black Barons responded, winning three of the next four games. Nashville, Monroe, and Indianapolis were next on the schedule to visit Rickwood in May, but rain washed out most of the first two series.

By the end of June, the league was in trouble. Teams couldn't afford to travel; some couldn't pay players. As clubs started to drop out, league officials attempted to prop up the circuit, but to no avail. By the end of August, the league had failed. Quoted in the *Chicago Defender*, Candy Jim Taylor said the Negro Southern League "had ceased to function since the end of the first half."

Bad luck and stormy weather plagued the Birmingham club in 1932. With the death of popular manager Geechie Meredith, the collapse of two leagues, and simply rainy day after rainy day, the team was overwhelmed with challenges on and off the field.

1933: Birmingham Benched

The Negro National League reformed, and the NSL was again refurbished. However, Birmingham was conspicuously absent from both. There were reports of the "Black Barons" in articles, as local clubs tried to gain notice by using the well-known moniker. The name "Black Barons" had become synonymous with Birmingham's team. The Birmingham Industrial League was the only game in town with Black professional baseball in the Steel City forced to the bench.

1934: The Barnstorming Giants

Determined to get back on the field, Frank Perdue attended NSL meetings representing Birmingham's interests. The league accepted his newly reminted Birmingham Giants. The league, however, was more of a loose agreement to schedule occasional games and refrain from poaching each other's players. The Birmingham Giants announced Bill Perkins as manager. It would be the first in a long series of vexing moves and announcements by the new organization. Perkins never showed up in reports. Paul Hardy was catching as early as mid-May and likely acted as manager.

Jerry Benjamin, a Montgomery native, was a three-time All-Star and won eight pennants while with the Homestead Grays. *Dr. Layton Revel/ Negro Southern League Museum.*

As spring began, fans were excited about Birmingham abandoning its Sunday baseball ban. The Giants brought back former Black Barons such as "Lick" Carlisle, "Jabbo" Andrews, and John Washington. Former Montgomery players Lefty Glover, Bill Perkins, and Matt Jackson were there. New centerfielder Jerry Benjamin was a Montgomery native who would have a long career with many teams.

The season began with a May 20 doubleheader win over Memphis and then games across Georgia. Once at home, they hosted Kansas City, winning twice but losing to former Black Baron Charlie Beverly.

A trip to St. Louis and Cincinnati, with a stop in Memphis, led the Birmingham Giants summer off. It was a road trip that would seemingly never end. After dropping two games in St. Louis, in Memphis the Birmingham Giants won 10–0 to open the series. The crowd was estimated at just 250, mostly boisterous women taking advantage of free admission on Ladies Night. The Giants then lost the next two games to the Red Sox. In Cincy, the Birmingham Giants split a series with the Tigers at Crosley Field and in nearby Hamilton, Ohio.

CHAPTER 12

RETURN OF THE BLACK BARONS

The Giants were suddenly billed as the Black Barons for barnstorming games against Homestead, becoming touring partners with Cum Posey's powerful Grays featuring Buck Leonard and former BBBs such as Harry Salmon. On June 24, Homestead's Harry Salmon shut out his old team, limiting Birmingham to just two hits. Starting in Ohio, the two clubs worked their way east to Maryland.

Birmingham then trekked back to Ohio after the Fourth of July to oppose the Cincinnati Tigers. In the first game of a doubleheader at Crosley Field, Birmingham tallied the game's only run when shortstop Benjamin singled, stole second, moved to third on a wild pitch, and scored when pitcher Porter Moss balked by dropping the ball while winding up.

Birmingham, once again the "Black Barons," traveled with a portable lighting system the *Titusville Herald* described as "of the latest style and is said to provide an unusual brilliance" for an August exhibition against the Penn-Drakes in Pennsylvania. The article also noted that the Birmingham club was managed by left-handed pitcher Dazzy Vance, likely pitcher Columbus Vance.

Enter Gus Greenlee

Birmingham was now under the direction of Gus Greenlee. Greenlee, also owner of the Pittsburgh Crawfords and president of the Negro National

A 1933 Pittsburgh Crawfords promotional poster, with owner Gus Greenlee and stars including Sam Streeter. *Author's collection.*

League, was a businessman, promoter, and philanthropist. Greenlee's Crawford Grille was the heart of Pittsburgh's bustling jazz music scene. Greenlee was also a racketeer, widely known as a numbers banker. Greenlee had led the relaunching of the NNL, and his stewardship of the Black Barons provided instant financial stability.

Working under Greenlee meant few home dates. However, Greenlee gave the Black Barons a lifeline during hard times. While other teams struggled to pay players, Birmingham was touring with the latest lighting innovations and establishing the Black Barons' reputation. The Black Barons barnstormed far and wide, from Pennsylvania to Louisiana. The St. Louis Stars were often opponents in smaller northern towns; local teams such as Canton's Cozy Clothiers also faced off against Birmingham during the tour. One game against Greenlee's Pittsburgh Crawfords started at midnight to showcase the portable lighting system.

The Black Barons closed the season in Monroe, Louisiana, where it was said that the team would play winter ball in California. No final standings were produced for the NSL.

1935: Black Barons Return to NSL (Again)

A preseason article in the *Atlanta Daily World* tabbed Gus Allen as owner and Molton Gray as business secretary. Allen was a former Pittsburgh boxer and numbers banker with obvious Greenlee connections. Molton Gray was a prominent Birmingham promoter.

Birmingham was back in the Negro Southern League under the familiar Black Barons name, with veteran catcher Poindexter Williams appointed manager. George McAllister returned, as did pitcher George Nash and outfielder Hamp Johnson, but they were the only ones who had appeared with Birmingham previously. The rest were new to the team, fresh-faced youngsters and Industrial League veterans. New leftfielder "Cat" Mays would be one of the top hitters in the lineup, although his son Willie would later outshine him.

The first exhibition game heralded the return of the Black Barons, and admission went up to forty cents. The Black Barons opened the season in Montgomery's Cramton Bowl against Candy Jim Taylor's Nashville Elite Giants. It would be the start of a rough ride.

Birmingham lost the opener in Montgomery and then lost at home. Beginning in May, the Black Barons faced Nashville in Montgomery and at Rickwood, with scores unreported and one game canceled. They headed to New Orleans, where they dropped a doubleheader. The club did well at home against Memphis but then kicked three games in Memphis.

First baseman Jabbo Andrews was reported managing as the Black Barons grabbed two wins in Atlanta. They were swept in Memphis, beaten in Atlanta, and then went back to Memphis, where they got more of the same. It was announced that George McAllister replaced Poindexter Williams as manager, with no mention of Andrews. However, that was among the last announcements. Games went unreported, and even home appearances were overlooked in local sports pages. They were dropping out of Birmingham newspapers, and other cities offered only occasional reports. An early August mention placed them facing the St. Louis Stars in Indiana. At the end of the month, they played the Grey Sox in Montgomery. The Black Barons closed the season against industrial teams.

The NSL was a loose organization; its fluidity offered it survival amid turmoil but often left everyone in the dark about stats, standings, and rosters. No final league numbers were produced.

1936: Andrew Walker's Black Barons

The Black Barons returned for '36 with Andrew Walker as manager, under new owner Alfreda Walker. The leadership is dubious. Andrew Walker was hailed as a local when the Black Barons played in Marion, Alabama, but very little is available on him. Even less is known about "owner" Alfreda Walker.

Historians label Andrew Walker as a likely numbers racketeer associated with various underworld figures. Birmingham reporter Emory O. Jackson later discussed Walker's connection with the team and questionable associations. Jackson, a respected newsman, blamed Walker for selling the Black Barons to Gus Greenlee, fragmenting the Birmingham team by sending its players to other teams. Historian William Plott disputed some details of Jackson's recollection, which Jackson wrote much later. Plott noted that the fragmentation took place in 1938, two years after Jackson places the event. Both are correct. Greenlee financed the Black Barons as early as '34, leading to the 1936 takeover that raised Jackon's ire. Later, Greenlee was plagued by financial issues, selling everything in 1938.

With Gus Greenlee holding financial control of the team, he either chose or approved Walker. Greenlee also wielded the same powers over the New Orleans Crescents and Memphis Red Sox. Memphis, New Orleans, and Birmingham issued nearly identical press releases identifying them as "under the direction of Gus Greenlee." Greenlee and his backers were controlling three top Black baseball teams in the South, as well as the Negro National League.

Whoever he was, Andrew Walker was the boss when spring camp started at Sloss Field. The Black Barons were infused with cash and riding in style. Birmingham now enjoyed its own bus for travel and sported new uniforms. Birmingham was back in the Negro Southern League, along with Montgomery. In classic NSL style, a schedule was released, but no teams adhered to it.

The Black Barons' season began against Nashville's Black Vols at Rickwood in front of a modest crowd of 3,500 fans. The opening day lineup had familiar Dewitt Owens in centerfield, Parnell Woods at third base, and Fred Bankhead at second. Newcomer David Whatley, added just before the start of the season, contributed two hits in the opening game. Fans enjoyed a 4–1 Birmingham victory as pitcher Jeff Posey struck out seven, and the team rolled into the new season, winning several series.

Facing Atlanta, Birmingham owned a sparkling record of 14-4. The team was playing well, and fans took note, as more than five thousand filled the Rickwood stands for Sunday's game. When the series shifted to Atlanta, a night game against the Black Crackers was the first time Black teams had played under lights at Ponce de Leon Park.

On May 31, Birmingham came home as a first-place team. For their doubleheader against Memphis, manager Walker chose Jack "Dizzy" Bruton and his brother Pit "Daffy" Bruton as pitchers. With nicknames borrowed from the St. Louis Cardinals pitchers, the Brutons pitched like the famous Gas House Gang siblings, winning both games.

The Black Barons then took their show to the people across the Black Belt region of Alabama. Selma, Greensboro, Marion, Uniontown, and Montgomery packed the ballparks to watch their local teams take on the now-famous Black Barons.

Their return to Rickwood brought Montgomery for a series that included a night game, misleadingly billed as the "first night game" between Black teams in Birmingham. That Monday night belonged to Montgomery's Lefty Glover, who struck out seventeen Black Barons, opening the game with ten strikeouts against the first twelve hitters.

The Black Barons stopped in Memphis for the July 4 series, won three times, and claimed the NSL first half flag. A schedule was released for the second half of the season, but in true NSL fashion, it did not include all the teams from the first half.

To open the second half, the Black Barons hosted Chattanooga; Daffy Bruton got the win. Lefty Glover was acquired from Montgomery, donned Birmingham togs, and struck out eight in three innings of relief. Jim Canada had three hits, also announcing his arrival to the team.

Birmingham hit the road to Jacksonville (Florida) and Nashville, where a July game was canceled, leading to a rumor the team had folded. When the club got home, they found Rickwood Field occupied by an amateur tournament. After the Black Barons convinced management that the rumors of their demise were greatly exaggerated, they regained possession of their home field in time to split a doubleheader with Memphis. Then the league-leading Black Barons went back out on the road, barnstorming across the region.

On August 16, Birmingham faced the New Orleans Cubans in a Rickwood doubleheader. The Black Barons took both contests behind pitchers Lefty Glover and Pit Bruton, aided by Jack "Dizzy" Bruton's two-run homer in game one.

Games against Clanton and Marion replaced a canceled barnstorming tour of the Northeast. As was often the case, NSL final standings were not compiled. After the season, the league folded.

BBBs Join Negro American League, Slip into Silence

With the creation of the Negro American League (by Gus Greenlee), the Black Barons found a stable partner and familiar opponents. It was a return to the major leagues.

Andrew Walker attended league meetings representing Birmingham in the new loop. Listed as owner at the meetings, Walker was repeatedly mentioned as being "appointed manager" by unnamed ownership during the spring. The *Birmingham-Post Herald* noted that "new capital was added" over the winter.

The team trained at Birmingham's Sloss Field, near the Sloss Furnace industrial plant. Fred Bankhead, one of five Bankhead brothers to play pro

DIZZY DISMUKES

William "Dizzy" Dismukes was born in Birmingham in 1890, where the Dismukeses were the first Black family in town to have a brick house. After leaving high school, he attended Tuskegee University, where he played on the school baseball team.

Dismukes was the first American athlete known by the nickname Dizzy, although his attitude was studious, disciplined, and businesslike. It was his pitching that earned him his nickname, as Dismukes baffled hitters with his submarine delivery, and his talents were in high demand. Working for Midwestern teams found Dismukes with Indianapolis, where he faced C.I. Taylor's Birmingham Giants for a 1909 game. Following the contest, Taylor told Dismukes, "Someday I am going to have you on my ball club."

While in St. Louis the very next year, Dismukes encountered C.I. Taylor, who informed him of the Birmingham Giants' relocation and invited Dismukes to join Taylor's new West Baden Sprudels. Dizzy would pitch for two years with Taylor's Sprudels, earning seventy-five dollars per month. With West Baden, Dismukes defeated the white Pittsburgh Pirates, 2–1, in a 1911 exhibition game.

Birmingham-born William "Dizzy" Dismukes, with the West Baden Sprudels. *Author's collection.*

After West Baden, Dismukes pitched in Florida with the Royal Poinciana Hotel, where he played with Henry Hannon. Pitching for Taylor's Indianapolis ABCs in 1915, Dismukes threw a no-hitter against Rube Foster's Chicago Giants.

Always a nomad, Dismukes was player/manager for many teams, including the Lincoln Stars, where he was paired with Louis Santop, leading to his first trip to Cuba. During World War I, Dismukes served in the Army and managed the only Black team in the service league in Nantes, France. After the war, Dizzy organized the

Dizzy Dismukes (*standing, third from right*), circa 1910, with Hall of Famer Pete Hill (*standing, second from right*), Charles Taylor (*kneeling, center in front with unknown child*), and Cannonball Dick Redding (*kneeling, front right*). *Author's collection.*

Pittsburgh Keystones, who were admitted to the NNL in 1922. Also in 1922, Dismukes began his journalism career, writing columns for the *Pittsburgh Courier* through the 1940s.

Following the death of his friend C.I. Taylor, Dismukes took over as manager of Taylor's Indianapolis ABCs in 1923. After two seasons, he then managed the Memphis Red Sox. When Rube Foster died, Dismukes was appointed manager of Foster's Chicago Giants.

Dismukes was a talented front office member for the St. Louis Stars for six seasons starting in 1926. As the Kansas City Monarchs team secretary, Dismukes signed talent such as Jackie Robinson, Ernie Banks, and Elston Howard. During the 1950s, Dizzy worked as a scout for the New York Yankees and Chicago Cubs.

When William "Dizzy" Dismukes passed away in 1961, he was hailed as a "baseball immortal," and his exploits were praised as being on par with Ty Cobb, Rube Foster, and Josh Gibson as among the greatest players in the game.

baseball, was among the returning Black Barons. Pitchers Dizzy and Daffy Bruton were back, as was slugging speedster David Whatley.

Opening day at Rickwood pitted them against Candy Jim Taylor's KC Monarchs, who scored seventeen runs in a doubleheader to spoil the occasion for the modest crowd of three thousand. The next guests were Dizzy Dismukes's St. Louis Stars. The Black Barons got the better of St. Louis but found little success afterward. Their home performance was uninspiring, losing to nearly every guest.

As the season progressed, the Black Barons slipped from the sports pages. In the *Atlanta Daily World*, sportswriter Emory O. Jackson laid the blame squarely on Andrew Walker, noting that the Black Barons offered less information than even sandlot teams. Jackson went farther, implying that secrecy was deliberate while cryptically saying, "While we desist from exposing, being hesitant to even criticize, we shall not stay silent on things for the sake of being gentle and helpful."

Barnstorming the Midwest, they played for big crowds. In Chicago, more than eight thousand fans filled the stands. Pitcher Lefty Craig was added as Birmingham's roster was revamped midseason in an effort to jumpstart the club.

The tour included the Duffy Florals of Chicago, where "Hammer Man" Whatley's two homers ended the florists' twenty-one-game winning streak. Green Bay's Green Sox and Sioux City's Cowboys also hosted the barnstorming Black Barons, who were now reported as promoted by Abe Saperstein. Saperstein was the force behind the Harlem Globetrotters basketball team. This would likely have been viewed by Greenlee as Saperstein encroaching on his turf, leading to front office friction as the Black Barons tried to make ends meet while appeasing two rival promoters.

The Black Barons finished in sixth place, well out of contention. David Whatley batted .396, second in the league.

BBBs Land New "Owner"

A new owner was announced for the Birmingham Black Barons. Henry Moore of Mississippi had previously owned the St. Louis Stars. He brought Dizzy Dismukes to manage, and several St. Louis Stars followed their former manager Dismukes to Birmingham. David Whatley returned to the top of the lineup, and Fred Bankhead, Parnell Woods, Alonzo "Hooks" Mitchell, and Jack "Dizzy" Bruton were back. Lester Lockett was among the new faces on the roster.

Opening day brought the Chicago Giants and star outfielder Turkey Stearnes to Rickwood, drawing more than four thousand fans who saw the Giants win the doubleheader 5–0 and 6–1.

A trip to Jacksonville began a tough stretch. After a pair of losses, they dropped three of four games in Atlanta. After struggling through a home series against Atlanta, they headed out on the road again, losing to Indianapolis and the Monarchs.

Birmingham had a firm grip on last place. Injuries began to mount, and a new shortstop was found in "Ground Hog" Cephus, who was under five feet tall. New first baseman Red Moore was garnering praise for his glovework.

In June, the Black Barons took two from Memphis in a doubleheader and then lost two to Chicago. A doubleheader victory at home against Jacksonville's Red Caps closed the first half of the season.

As part of the July 4 game in Chicago, Birmingham's David Whatley outran Olympian Jesse Owens in the hundred-yard dash. Whatley was called the "fastest man in the Negro Leagues" by many. August 16 was a career day for David Whatley. Facing St. Louis, the Black Barons plated ten in the first inning as Whatley went six for six, hitting for the cycle with two doubles on the day.

The club showed flashes of excellence but was never in contention. In spite of the poor showing in the standings, Birmingham was chosen to be part of a four-team doubleheader showcase in New York, an idea by Abe Saperstein. Birmingham faced Newark at Yankee Stadium in the first game. More than eighteen thousand were on hand when former Black Baron Mule Suttles hit a three-run homer to beat Birmingham, 6–2.

The East-West All-Star Game at Comiskey Park included Parnell Woods on August 21, the first Black Baron in the annual contest.

The season closed with losses to Kansas City; the final two Rickwood contests were canceled due to small crowds. The team cited "financial difficulties," and the lost games threw a wrench into the standings and forced loop president R.R. Jackson to determine a champion well after the season.

In an October All-Star Game in New York, Birmingham's Dizzy Bruton walked in the winning run of the contest, held at the Polo Grounds in front of more than fifteen thousand fans.

Of the '38 Black Barons, Birmingham newsman Emory O. Jackson said, "They passed bad checks, were hunted by the tax collector, their gate receipts were twice attached. They lost their bus, some players and their last game."

1939: No More Moore

Henry Moore did not field a 1939 team. Moore was suspended by the league, and his franchise was revoked for his role in organizing the Polo Grounds All-Star Game. By the time the league voted unanimously to uphold Moore's expulsion in December 1938, the team's two top stars, Whatley and Bankhead, had been sold to Memphis. The rest of the players were declared free agents, scattering them across baseball.

Some reports say that Moore sold the team to Gus Greenlee. Greenlee's control does much to explain the Black Barons' nomadic business plan and baffling roster decisions during the 1930s, although it's unlikely that

Sun-Telegraph Photo

PARTNER "WOOGIE"

They mortgaged houses, cars and jewelry . . .

Sun-Telegraph Photo

PARTNER "GUS"

. . . to pay off on the dreaded 805 "hit."

Gus Greenlee and his partner "Woogie" Harris were deeply involved in the numbers racket. *From the Bulletin Index, February 1936, courtesy of the Pittsburgh Gazette.*

he purchased the team in 1938. Greenlee, who appears to have owned the Black Barons in every way except on paper since at least 1934, had a financial crisis during 1938. Rumored to be facing a big numbers payout and dogged by taxes and other problems, Greenlee liquidated his interests. Moore's expulsion was likely the Negro American League further distancing itself from its former president's influence.

Black Barons' new owner Tom Hayes Jr. also purchased Birmingham's Rush Hotel, where visiting teams lodged. *Memphis and Shelby County Room, Memphis Public Libraries.*

The punishment was overly harsh in the opinion of league secretary Cum Posey, who shared in his column in the *New Pittsburgh Courier* in October 1938. As owner of the Homestead Grays, however, Posey voted in favor of upholding the suspension a few weeks later. Posey's business partner was Pittsburgh numbers racketeer "Sonnyman" Jackson, a Greenlee rival.

In December 1939, Mississippi undertaker Thomas Hayes Jr. purchased the team's franchise from the league and secured Rickwood Field for use.

CHAPTER 13

ENTER THE HOUSE OF MOSES

Two teams, or perhaps one Jekyll/Hyde team using a barnstorming name for non-league action, dominated Montgomery ballfields in the 1930s, competing for top billing, sharing players, and mysteriously never quite facing each other.

In Montgomery, Earl "Curley" Gurley was appointed the House of Moses manager for the 1933 season by club president Jesse Gosha, who was connected to the Grey Sox. Listed sometimes as George or James, Gurley was a Tennessean who had played with Chicago and Birmingham.

Baseball stadium view at Alabama State University, the home field for the Montgomery Grey Sox and the House of Moses in the 1930s. *Alabama State University.*

Tuskegee baseball team, 1940s. *Estate of Willy M. Jackson.*

Later in the summer, playing at College Hill Park, the House of Moses added former unnamed Grey Sox players, quickly becoming one of the stronger teams in the area.

The Grey Sox and House of Moses announced an April doubleheader. The Moses were undefeated, boasting a string of eight consecutive victories ahead of the rivalry games with the Grey Sox. A large crowd was expected,

with special seating for white fans. Unfortunately, if the game occurred, no results were publicized.

The House of Moses played the Tuskegee Veterans Black Socks at Tuskegee's Shady Nook Park on May 20 in an extra-inning affair, with Moses pitcher Lawyer Chattman facing the Tuskegee starter, Cunningham. It took twelve innings before the House of Moses prevailed 5–4. In September, the House of Moses and Tuskegee met again for two games in Montgomery. The House of Moses won both behind pitchers Roe and Botee.

1933: Grey Sox's NSL Return

Montgomery's Grey Sox returned to the Negro Southern League for the second half of the season, replacing Monroe, Louisiana. The NSL, however, was back to being a minor league. Most Grey Sox players were noted only by last name. Among them was a catcher who had been with the House of Moses, listed as "Ed. Tyson"; this was likely Armand "Cap" Tyson, who would later appear with Birmingham. Grey Sox infielder Lennon Henderson was a veteran of top southern clubs.

The Grey Sox hosted Louisville for a July 3 doubleheader and posted one of the most lopsided scores in local history, winning both games by a combined 30–2.

A few days later, on July 9, Grey Sox starting pitcher Lefty Glover tallied twenty strikeouts in a game held at Cramton Bowl against Little Rock, setting a Montgomery record for strikeouts in a game that has stood for nearly a century.

In late July, Montgomery won five times in Athens, Georgia, in one game defeating Athens in an eighteen-inning marathon. It was the third extra-inning Grey Sox game in four days.

Montgomery native Thomas "Lefty" Glover-Moss was the starting pitcher for the 1945 East-West All-Star Game. *Courtesy of Gary Cieradkowski.*

Lefty Glover

The Grey Sox ace was Thomas "Lefty" Glover-Moss. Born in 1911 in Montgomery County, Alabama, Thomas Glover-Moss was a talented young pitcher who played with clubs such as Birmingham's Black Barons and Baltimore's Elite Giants, as well as in Mexico. Lefty Glover pitched several excellent games for Montgomery this season, including one in which he beat Chicago by allowing just four hits. With his reliable curveball, Glover had a successful career until his untimely death from tuberculosis in 1948 at the age of thirty-seven. Lefty Glover still holds the Montgomery record for most strikeouts in a single game with twenty and the most consecutive strikeouts in a game with ten.

1934: Grey Sox Wash Out, House of Moses In

Montgomery was excluded from the Negro Southern League, and there were no reports of Grey Sox games during this season. Part of the issue may have been the condition of College Hill Park, as the *Atlanta Daily World* reported in January that the ballpark fencing and grandstand had "taken the blues and walked away," requiring replacement.

In March, the House of Moses prepared for spring games bolstered by at least four former Grey Sox. Henderson, Pennington, Johnson, and Lamar were Grey Sox and now with the Moses. "Bare" Owens was the star, as manager Gosha declared his House of Moses a "red hot team this year."

1935: Grey Sox Slipping and Moses Falls Silent

The Montgomery Grey Sox returned to action in '35. Their roster included only a few players with first names known, including first baseman and manager Earl Gurley, catcher Paul Hardy, pitcher Joe Turner, and left fielder Edgar Pool. Former Bama State star Atkin Collins, Burke, and Stokes pitched for Montgomery. The team was promoted and sometimes managed by Willie Brown.

The Grey Sox barnstormed Alabama, Georgia, and Florida, and their games at Cramton Bowl still drew nice crowds. One report from Greenville, however, showed Montgomery being struck out twelve times in defeat, a sign that the Grey Sox were sometimes overwhelmed by lesser teams. Other reports indicated that the Sox were struggling financially, saying they were eager to visit Atlanta in order to earn much-needed fluidity. Claiming twenty-eight wins and eleven losses through the start of August, the Montgomery Grey Sox were showing signs of fatigue.

The House of Moses was conspicuously absent from the 1935 season, with no reports.

1936: Grey Sox Open Park, Taunt Tigers, Face Zulus

The Montgomery Grey Sox were back with catcher Paul Hardy managing and Willie Brown as team president. They found a new home on North

Decatur Street, financed by Brown on land where Camp Sheridan had been. Ace pitcher Lefty Glover was tabbed for the opening day start to christen the new ballpark. A "Name the Park" contest was held, offering a five-dollar prize for the fan submitting the winning name. The winning name chosen was Brown's Park.

In June, Lefty Glover struck out seventeen batters in a night game against the Black Barons at Rickwood Field. The Grey Sox won 14–8. Lefty Glover struck out ten of the first twelve hitters to face him but tired late and allowed eight runs in the victory.

The Grey Sox, who relied on their star pitcher Lefty Glover, dealt him to Birmingham midseason, presumably for cash. In August, the team sold its starting shortstop, Clarence Lamar, to the St. Louis Giants. At the time of the deal, Lamar was among the Grey Sox leaders in home runs and stolen bases.

Along the same lines, Montgomery's best prospect, switch-hitting infielder Howard Easterling (later a four-time Negro National League All-Star who would play in the World Series with Hilldale), was dealt midseason in a move that very quickly came back to hurt the Grey Sox.

Montgomery made a lengthy road trip across Kentucky, Ohio, Indiana, and Tennessee. Included was Cincinnati, where a rivalry was brewing with the Cincinnati Tigers, with former Montgomery Grey Sox infielder Howard Easterling and five native Alabamians rostered. The Grey Sox talked trash before arriving, declaring that the Cincy Tigers would be "easy meat" according to the *Cincinnati Enquirer*. The Grey Sox were swept by the Tigers at Cincinnati's Crosley Field.

While in Cincinnati, the Montgomery Grey Sox also faced off against, and were defeated by, the Zulu Cannibal Giants in Crosley Field. The Zulu Cannibals were generally considered a novelty act, one frowned upon by many African Americans. Promoted by white booking agent Syd Pollack, the Zulu Cannibal Giants capitalized on racial stereotypes of African tribal natives. Playing barefoot while wearing grass skirts and with faces striped with war paint, players used names such as "Impo" or "Limpopo." Zulu players were willing to clown for their paycheck but still hated to lose. After a few innings of goofy acts, including war dances and speaking in gibberish, players would take up the game in earnest, abandoning the tribal shtick.

On June 1, the Grey Sox won a thriller over the Black Crackers in front of more than two thousand fans at Ponce de Leon Park. Grey Sox third baseman Carter had three hits, and Montgomery escaped a ninth-inning jam to win.

Syd Pollack's Zulu team relied on imposing costumes and on-field antics. *Postcard courtesy of Leon Luckey.*

The Grey Sox turned a triple play at Atlanta's Ponce de Leon Park on June 4. In the seventh inning, with the bases loaded and no outs, a hot line drive was speared by Montgomery shortstop Nichols, who stepped on second to double off the runner and threw to first base to complete the rare play. Montgomery, however, lost the game.

The Grey Sox and Black Barons played the first night game between Black teams at Rickwood Field on June 17. It was the first season that the Birmingham ballpark, opened in 1910, had lights. The Grey Sox were used to night games, as Montgomery's Cramton Bowl installed lights in 1927 and hosted Grey Sox night games beginning in 1930.

The Grey Sox promoted a three-game rivalry series with the House of Moses in June, but no game reports were issued.

The Grey Sox claimed the league lead in July after beating Chattanooga five straight. However, Montgomery registered a paltry 4-15 record in "official" games before the league's midseason collapse. No team completed the schedule; no final standings were produced. The NSL would not reform until after World War II.

1936–1939: Return of the House of Moses

The House of Moses reappeared in 1936, hosting the Zulu Cannibals and visiting Miami and Columbus, Georgia. The House of Moses played as an independent club, garnering a reputation for quality talent. Pitcher "Lefty" Grieg, sometimes spelled "Craig," was the staff ace.

1937: Montgomery Grey Sox Fade

The Grey Sox faded from the scene. Ownership had changed multiple times; the team was possibly connected to the original club by name only. Reports indicated that the Grey Sox traveled to Knoxville. However, both Knoxville newspapers referred to the team as the "Montgomery Grey Sox of Moses, Tennessee." There is no city of Moses in Tennessee. The Grey Sox name was also used by a Monsanto Mills team.

1939: Josh Gibson Visits Selma, Montgomery Cheers Black Yankees

Selma's Rowell Field welcomed Josh Gibson's Homestead Grays and the Atlanta Black Crackers on April 28. Atlanta's infielder Jabbo Andrews, from Dallas County, rapped three hits, including a triple and home run, in front of his hometown crowd. Atlanta defeated the Grays, 5–3. Atlanta's Black Crackers were back in Selma on June 21, hosting the Memphis Red Sox at Rowell Field. Memphis pitcher Lefty Wilson tossed a two-hit shutout to win 4–0.

Montgomery's Cramton Bowl hosted New York's Black Yankees and the Baltimore Elite Giants. More than two thousand fans turned out on August 3 as the Black Yankees defeated Baltimore, 4–2. The Black Yankees were managed by former Grey Sox infielder George Scales. Yankees starting pitcher Terris McDuffie outdueled the Elites hurler Emery Adams. Soon after, on September 12, Cramton Bowl hosted the Kansas City Monarchs against the Memphis Red Sox. Hilton Smith tossed a complete game for the Monarchs, downing Memphis, 12–3.

1930s Baseball Across Alabama

Elba's newspaper gave good coverage to its team. Elba's tie with Troy was front-page news in the *Elba Clipper* in July 1931. A 15–0 victory over Glenwood a week later only made it to page 4.

Anniston's Grey Sox hosted the Newnan (Georgia) Grey Sox in 1931 at Fair Park.

The Anniston Yellowjackets faced industrial teams at the Silver Run Farmers' diamond in '32.

Red Bay opposed Moulton in Haleyville in '32. The winner then played the host city's team managed by Sam Knox; admission was ten cents.

The Hartselle Hawks and Moulton Tigers were a popular rivalry, and their '32 lineups included local stars such as Hartselle's Toney Pruitt and Moulton's Fowler brothers. Moulton boasted a 20-3 record in 1930.

Evergreen played Andalusia and Brewton in 1932. Willie Lloyd, Wilson Cross, and Sim Brown were well-known Evergreen Black Sox players.

The Montgomery Blue Caps were among the teams in Montgomery's competitive city league. Based in Washington Park, the Blue Caps were led by former ASU Hornets football star Mizell Stewart.

J.C. Weeks of Elba struck out twenty-two Brundige batters in a shutout on June 25, 1934. The next week, he punched out seventeen more Brundige hitters.

The Roanoke Tigers held a doubleheader with LaGrange's Black Caps on Independence Day 1934.

Greenville's Black Sox of '35 featured pitcher Marbury "the Colored Dizzy Dean," who shut out New Orleans' Black Pelicans and beat the Montgomery Grey Sox with a homer and twelve strikeouts.

Local teams such as Flomaton's Century Giants, the Jasper Tigers, and the Atmore Blackcats were very popular. Even the Dooley Ditch team attracted hundreds of fans for games near Anniston's city hall in 1936.

The Bevelle Black Crackers beat three teams in one week at the new Turner Field in Alex City, downing Shawmut, the Alex City Reds, and Lanett's Black Caps in 1938.

Manager C.W. Boone led his Lanett Black Caps in games at Jackson Hill Park. In 1939, they became the Lanett Black Panthers.

Troy's Black Caps (also called the Thunderbolts) faced Crenshaw County's Luverne Cats in 1939. Troy was managed by James Harris.

CHAPTER 14

1940s WARTIME BASEBALL RATIONS IN MONTGOMERY

Baseball was eagerly supported across Alabama. Without a league club, Montgomery's spacious Cramton Bowl became a popular site for hosting barnstorming teams.

Satchel Paige's All-Stars made a much-anticipated visit to Montgomery's Cramton Bowl, facing Brooklyn's Royal Giants on May 27, 1940. Satchel pitched in relief but allowed the go-ahead run in the ninth inning, and Paige's All-Stars were defeated 5–4 in front of a huge crowd. Admission was forty cents, the usual fare for baseball at the Bowl.

Cramton Bowl hosted the Black Barons and Cleveland Bears in a night exhibition game on May 3. The Bears won 9–4, but the feature of the night was an impressive home run by Birmingham's "Jabbo" Andrews.

In August, the New York Black Yankees and Baltimore Elite Giants faced off in two games at Cramton Bowl. Montgomery fans declared the second game "Johnny Washington Night" to honor the Black Yankees star infielder. A Montgomery native, Washington responded with two hits in each game to lead New York to two victories. Also with the Black Yanks was George "Tubby" Scales. Future Hall of Famer Roy Campanella was catching for Baltimore, leading the Elites with two hits in each game.

Johnny Washington

When John G. Washington played his first professional game with the Montgomery Grey Sox in 1933, he was just seventeen years old. Returning to Montgomery in 1940, he was among the top players in baseball. Impressing first with Montgomery, Johnny then appeared with Birmingham's Black Barons before joining Pittsburgh. A backup at first base behind Oscar Charleston with the Crawfords, Washington earned his first All-Star selection in 1936.

After the Black Yankees acquired him for 1939, John Washington led the league with a .377 batting average. Primarily a first baseman, Washington spent four years in military service before returning with the Baltimore Elite Giants. Johnny Washington played three more seasons at the top level and in Cuba, where he earned another All-Star selection.

John Washington was the All-Star starter at first base for the East division in '47 and an All-Star yet again in 1950, serving as backup first sacker. In all, John Washington was a three-time NNL All-Star and a Negro National League batting champion. He led the league in singles in 1941 and triples in 1936. John Washington passed away in Detroit in 1983.

1940: Grey Sox and House of Moses Still Standing

In May, the Grey Sox were in Columbus, Georgia, facing the strong Twenty-Fourth Infantry team from Fort Benning. The Grey Sox dropped the first game, 3–2. In game two, the Grey Sox were embarrassed, losing 25–0 and striking out sixteen times as they were no-hit by the Army team. Game three wasn't much better for Montgomery, who were skunked 23–1; the Infantry swept the series. The teams met again at Browns Park in Montgomery for three games the following week, billed as "Frank Johnson's" Montgomery Grey Sox for its top slugger.

The Grey Sox dropped a June doubleheader to Union Springs' Red Birds, with both games going ten innings. In July, the Grey Sox returned the favor, sweeping the Red Birds in a pair of games at Union Springs. Other trips included Meridian, Mississippi, where the Grey Sox won a doubleheader.

The House of Moses returned to action, playing the Troy Thunderbolts team at Troy. The House of Moses also faced the Union Springs Red Birds and hosted the Tuskegee Faculty All-Stars in games at Browns Park.

Giants and Buckeye Browns Rule City League

The Montgomery Giants began taking on clubs from Troy and Union Springs in 1940. By the following season, the Giants were playing in front of large crowds at Brown's Park, featuring pitcher "Smoke Ball" Young. George "Smoke Ball" Young was the ace of the Giants staff. The rest of the Montgomery Giants pitching comprised George Edwards, Jackson, Scrubbs, and Cheatham. Burkette was a playing manager for the Giants, handling catching duties along with John Morgan and Carvin Crowe. The Giants outfield starred Rosevelt, Fanning, and Mitchell, with W. Haywood also being listed as occasional manager. On the infield, Chapel, Morgan, and Grant were the highlights.

One of the better teams in the Montgomery city league, the Buckeye Browns were noted for strong pitching and repeated defeats doled out to tough industrial teams. Sometimes facing Selma, Decatur, Greenville, and other area clubs, the Buckeye Browns held their own at Brown's Park. In 1940, the Buckeye Browns and Montgomery Grey Sox faced off in a June doubleheader benefiting Hale Infirmary. The game featured many local stars in the lineups. The Grey Sox manhandled the Buckeye Browns in both games, 7–4 and 22–5.

Montgomery's Buckeye Browns were managed by S.P. Owens. Pitchers "Steel Arm" Lefty Turner, Plug "Mystery Ball" Brinson, "Bullet Arm" Nelson, and PeeWee Owens led the staff. Jack Boyd, "Dead Shot" Hall, and "Death Blow" Leroy were catchers with the team.

Two unidentified Montgomery Giants players in the only known photo of the team, circa 1940s. *Author's collection.*

The year 1941 found the Buckeye Browns competing in a hotly contested Montgomery city league finals against the Montgomery Giants. The rivalry was evidenced by a midseason doubleheader billed as the local East-West Games, with the Giants representing Montgomery's east side and the Buckeye Browns repping the west side.

The Montgomery Giants ultimately won the title with a decisive 20–6 victory behind the pitching of George Young. The Giants were still managed by Burkette and W. Haywood. The club sported strong pitching, veteran catching, and swift outfielders. Montgomery Giants pitchers Scrubbs and Edwards each tossed shutouts for the Giants to help win the City League over the Buckeye Browns. Later articles said that the Montgomery Giants finished with a record of twenty-two wins, three losses, and one tie.

1942: Montgomery Grey Sox Finally Unravel

In May 1942, the Montgomery Grey Sox were beaten by the Montgomery Giants, 10–4, in what was described as a Negro City League contest. Pitcher George Edwards of the Giants allowed just four hits, and Stokes hit a home run for the Giants in a local battle of old versus new. It was the end of the line for the Montgomery Grey Sox, who seemingly vanished following their defeat to the Giants.

The Montgomery Giants barnstormed the area, facing Troy at Trojan Park in June. The Troy Tigers held the lead until George Edwards relieved the starting pitcher, Johns, after six innings. Edwards limited the Tigers to three hits and drove a home run over the wall to help the Giants to an 11–7 victory.

1943: Montgomery Enjoys Clowns, Barons, Giants, and Trustys

Teams were often shorthanded due to wartime enlistment, yet some remained active, and in 1943, the Cincinnati Clowns held their spring training in Montgomery. Hosting a pair of April exhibition games against Birmingham's Black Barons, the teams split the series, with Birmingham losing the first game to the Clowns pitcher George Daniels and winning the second contest behind starter Johnny Markham. The Birmingham Black Barons often called Montgomery their second home, as was evident in 1943 when the Black Barons played nearly a dozen games at Cramton Bowl.

In mid-May, the *Montgomery Advertiser* covered the Montgomery Giants' victory over the Maxwell Field Fourth Aviation Squadron and predicted that the Giants "will take another pennant this year as they have done the last two." The 1943 Giants were part of the USO league, built on the foundations of the City Leagues. Both white and Black local leagues composed of industrial

After years of long bus rides, Satchel later preferred driving himself to games in his maroon Cadillac. *Library of Congress, Prints & Photographs Division, FSA/OWI Collection.*

teams were met with player shortages, and many were replaced with military teams. The Montgomery Giants, the top team in the Black city league, were one of the few clubs to continue through the war.

The USO-sponsored league included the Montgomery Giants, the Montgomery Junior Giants, the Montgomery Reds, the Seeger Packing Company, the Montgomery Browns, the Montgomery Tigers, the Gunter Field Twenty-Second Aviation Squadron, Maxwell Field Fourth Aviation Squadron, the Bellair Greencaps, and the Capitol Trusty Club. The Greencaps were actual bellhops. The Trusty club was composed of prisoners from Prison Number 4 (now ALDOC Red Eagle Honor Farm) entrusted as laborers at the Alabama State Capitol.

Much of the nation was without baseball as World War II idled teams and leagues. Montgomery, however, was treated to some of the biggest names in baseball at Cramton Bowl on Monday nights. Contests featured teams such as the Chicago American Giants and the Kansas City Monarchs. A welcome wartime diversion, games sometimes filled Cramton Bowl near its capacity of eight thousand. Sections were also provided for white fans, and GIs were given free admission. Alabama Governor Chauncey Sparks and Montgomery Mayor Cy Brown attended, their seats draped with patriotic bunting. Often games included war bond promotions, bands, dances, contests, and other wartime related events. The popular Monday night games continued throughout the war.

Satchel Paige brought his KC Monarchs to Cramton Bowl in April to face his old team, the Birmingham Black Barons. Reports from that day said that Satchel "whizzed them by the Barons with plenty of zip" in his three innings.

MONTGOMERY'S BLACK REBELS

In 1944, the Black Rebels were formed by owner Hoyt Taylor, featuring local talent. The lineup was reported as Lawrence Whatley in left field, Fred Gilmer (sometimes "Gilbert") at third base, Junior "June" Johnson at first, shortstop Joe Bailey, Hoyt "Hagg" Taylor in centerfield, pitcher Willie George, Preston "Percy" Thomas playing right field, Levan Johnson as the catcher, and George Edwards handling second base. The Black Rebels hoped to generate interest for a new league in the area but found a home in the Georgia-Tennessee semipro circuit.

Or, alternatively, according to another reporter, "he didn't work, just went through the motions…throwing his nothing ball," offering conflicting views depending on which Montgomery newspaper report you read. The results were the same: the Black Barons lost to the Monarchs, 2–1.

Other contests in Montgomery during the summer of 1943 featured the Black Barons opposing the Chicago American Giants, Memphis Red Sox, Cincinnati Clowns, and New York Cubans.

Big Games at Montgomery in '44

The Birmingham Black Barons continued to host visitors at their home away from home, Cramton Bowl, often in Monday night matchups.

On April 10, Alfred Saylor pitched the Black Barons past the Cincinnati-Indianapolis Clowns, 5–1, in a Monday night contest. The following weekend, the New York Black Yankees faced the Baltimore Elite Giants in a Sunday doubleheader at Montgomery. The first game was a nine-inning tie, knotted at four apiece. In the second game, the Elite Giants beat the Black Yanks, 9–6.

The very next day, the Birmingham Black Barons fell to the New York Cubans, 6–2, at Cramton. Cuban Hall of Famer Luis Tiant Sr. tossed the final two frames for New York. In this game, Montgomery fans were treated to a classic performance by Mobile native Ted "Double Duty" Radcliffe of the Black Barons. After four innings of pitching, Ted did double duty and went behind the plate to catch the last five frames. Radcliffe, however, was saddled with the L after giving up three runs.

Cunningham was listed as the umpire for the contest between the NY Cubans and Black Barons. Marion "Dad" Cunningham, who lived near the ballpark, remained connected with the game throughout his life.

In their final Montgomery appearance of 1944, the Baltimore Elites defeated the Birmingham Black Barons, 3–2, on April 24 as Elites starting pitcher Andy "Pullman" Porter had a career day. Porter allowed just two hits to the Black Barons from the mound while collecting three knocks himself at the plate, including a homer and driving in all three of the Elites runs as a one-man wrecking crew.

The Kansas City Monarchs made three visits to Cramton Bowl in 1944, beginning with a May 15 game against Birmingham. More than two thousand fans were on hand to see the Black Barons' John Huber outpitch the Monarchs Jack Matchett under the lights, as Birmingham scored late to beat KC, 6–5.

The Monarchs matched up with the Cleveland Buckeyes, and Jack Matchett earned the victory as the Monarchs edged Cleveland, 5–4, on June 14. In July, the Monarchs were back in Montgomery, again facing the Black Barons. Birmingham starter Jimmy Newberry allowed just two runs as the Black Barons downed Kansas City, 6–2, in front of nearly three thousand spectators.

At the end of July, the Black Barons were in Montgomery facing the Chicago Giants. Chicago pounded out seventeen hits to beat Birmingham, 13–5. The next day, Black Barons starter Johnny Markham held Chicago to just one run on five hits. Birmingham won, 5–1, aided by three Giants errors. The Black Barons won twice more in Montgomery that summer, topping the Memphis Red Sox in August and besting the NY Cubans in September.

1945: Jackie Robinson Among Touring Teams in Montgomery

Jackie Robinson visited Montgomery with the Monarchs for an April exhibition series. Kansas City won both games, but local press largely ignored the UCLA star and nothing was published about Jackie's performance at Cramton Bowl. Former Montgomery Grey Sox infielder Johnny Ray was among the Monarchs, who defeated the Birmingham Black Barons in two non-league games.

In May 1945, Montgomery's Cramton Bowl was the location hosting the Birmingham Black Barons and the Indianapolis Clowns of Cincinnati for a pair of exhibition games. The Ethiopian Clowns were run by the same Sid Pollack who organized the Zulu team. They were promoted by Abe Saperstein, owner of the Harlem Globetrotters and promoter for Birmingham's Black Barons. The Clowns, like the Zulus, were often harshly disparaged by contemporaries for their clowning, with antics regarded as demeaning and detrimental to breaking racial stereotypes.

The Clowns would sometimes begin games with full clown attire, with face paint, wigs, and traditional clown costumes. The players clowned vocally and with exaggerated actions, using pantomime to entertain audiences. Once the game started, the Clowns pulled off their circus

Originally from Miami and then Cincinnati and finally Indianapolis, the Clowns were among the last functioning Negro League teams, barnstorming until 1989. *Indianapolis Clowns program from author's collection.*

costumes, revealing baseball uniforms underneath. As the game progressed, their clown faces became fearsome caricatures as the greasepaint smeared with sweat and dirt. Later, the team stuck with normal uniforms, but continued clowning acts would keep them active into the 1980s. The Clowns promised their full show in Montgomery, with a baseball comedy act including pregame shadowball, a pepper game, and stars King Tut and Ed Hammen performing between innings.

The Clowns clowned around and lost 9–3 to Birmingham at Cramton Bowl. The box score indicated that the Black Barons scored nine runs but had only one hit, which illustrates how the Clowns sometimes held entertainment value over the final score when games weren't being counted toward the league schedule.

The Cleveland Buckeyes took up residency at Montgomery for about a week in the late spring, playing three games at Cramton Bowl. They began by dispatching the Chicago Giants on May 1, 7–6, in front of more than two thousand fans behind Cleveland starter Willie Jefferson.

Then the Buckeyes faced the Birmingham Black Barons. Willie Jefferson again got the victory as the Buckeyes knocked off the Black Barons in game one by a 5–4 score, defeating Fay Washington. On the very next day, Tuesday, May 8, the Birmingham Black Barons won 4–2 over the Cleveland Buckeyes at Cramton Bowl in Montgomery. If no one noticed, it was because that was V-E Day, when the Axis powers in Europe surrendered to the Allies.

1945: All-Star Game Features Tuskegee Red Tails Airmen

Cramton Bowl was the site of the city league All-Star Game; the league was known as the V-J League in 1945. The home team consisted of the top nine city league players. Opposing them was the Tuskegee Army Airfield team, supported by their impressive fifty-six-piece Army band furnishing music during the contest. The Tuskegee team boasted veteran players from the Homestead Grays, Newark Eagles, Philadelphia Stars, Chicago Giants, Birmingham Black Barons, and others.

CHAPTER 15

1940s WARTIME BASEBALL RATIONS IN BIRMINGHAM

1940: Enter Abe Saperstein

Birmingham had yet another new owner, a new bus, and a new manager; Candy Jim Taylor skippered the Black Barons, training in owner Tom Hayes's native Jackson Mississippi.

The Mississippi mortician was a good fit as owner, but like Henry Moore before him, Tom Hayes was beholden to his partner. Hayes was in business with Abe Saperstein. Known best for his Harlem Globetrotters, Saperstein handled many sports entertainment acts. Like Greenlee, Saperstein had connections for booking games in large venues. Also like Greenlee, Saperstein already ran a baseball team, the Ethiopian Clowns. Unlike Gus Greenlee, however, Saperstein was not involved in organized crime. Journalist Emory O. Jackson noted in his *Atlanta Daily World* column that Birmingham's owners were a string of unsavory characters. Seven men after Joe Rush had owned the team, including "Charlie Johnson, notorious bootlegger; Albert 'Freddo' Walker, former number baron; [and] Gus Allen, former number king."

Abe Saperstein saved the Black Barons, funding an infusion of local talent after its recent dismantling and guaranteeing inclusion in top leagues. However, Saperstein's stewardship required long tours with little focus on Birmingham. Saperstein was also quick to appropriate talent, which was good for players' careers but taxed the club's depth.

Stars Jabbo Andrews, Dan Bankhead, and Jack Bruton joined many newcomers that included Lyman Bostock Sr. and Tommy Sampson.

Above: Birmingham owner Tom Hayes with the Black Barons' new bus at Rickwood Field. *Memphis and Shelby County Room, Memphis Public Libraries.*

Left: Promoter Abe Saperstein and Black Barons owner Tom H. Hayes. *Memphis and Shelby County Room, Memphis Public Libraries.*

Opposite: May 12, 1940 advertisement for the game between the Birmingham Black Barons and the Kansas City Monarchs in Selma, Alabama, from the *Selma Times.*

Manager Candy Jim Taylor pitched occasionally. In Nashville, he came in with the bases loaded and allowed just one run. Then the fifty-six-year-old tossed two more innings of scoreless relief.

The Monarchs were opening day opponents at Rickwood Field, shutting out the Black Barons, who won twice the next day but scuffled against St. Louis and Chicago before finally ending the skid by beating Memphis at

Rickwood. The Black Barons ventured to Selma to face the Monarchs and Anniston for a game at Johnston Park against the St. Louis–New Orleans Stars in May. Reports said that one thousand fans, Black and white, were in attendance as Birmingham lost, 13–2.

In June, the Black Barons returned to Anniston, beating the Cleveland Bears, 6–5. In between those contests, the Black Barons traveled to face the Memphis Red Sox in Gadsden, losing 2–1 under the lights. The new bus allowed more appearances within driving distance; even home series usually include games in other Alabama cities. Touring the country widely, they opposed local teams, independent clubs, and league opponents in any ballpark available. White teams were included, such as the Brooklyn Bushwicks.

When Toledo's Crawfords arrived, they were loaded with familiar faces. Formerly Gus Greenlee's Pittsburgh Crawfords, now under new ownership, they had absorbed many former Black Barons. The series featured guest appearances by Jesse Owens and rain. The Black Barons struggled to find traction. Chicago was the season's final home opponent, while skipper Taylor and two stars were at the All-Star Game in KC. Attendance was slipping, both at Rickwood and across the Negro Leagues. Monday games were abandoned due to low turnout.

In the offseason, the Black Barons barnstormed with Satchel Paige's All-Stars.

1941: Win Welch

Winfield Welch was named manager. A Saperstein employee, Welch managed Saperstein's Satchel Paige All-Stars and the Harlem Globetrotters basketball team, as well as a variety of other tasks. A strong core with catcher Paul Hardy, Lyman Bostock, Lester Lockett, and Tommy Sampson was rostered, as was popular Reese "Goose" Tatum. It's said that during a rainout, Goose Tatum was seen playing basketball, leading to his legendary career with Saperstein's Harlem Globetrotters.

Black Barons manager Winfield S. Welch (*on right*), with Ted "Double Duty" Radcliffe (*on left*) and Lloyd "Ducky" Davenport (*center*). *Memphis and Shelby County Room, Memphis Public Libraries.*

The Newark Eagles, featuring a young Mobile native named Monte Irvin, visited for a preseason series. The future Hall of Famer stole three bases in a doubleheader.

Rickwood's opening day brought Dizzy Dismukes's KC Monarchs to town. The rival Monarchs again spoiled the Black Barons' opener, pounding twenty-five hits in the doubleheader and winning easily.

Hitting the road, Birmingham reeled off a string of victories, running the total to eight straight. They faced the Decatur Tigers and KC Monarchs and then beat Jacksonville's Red Caps in Anniston. Hosting Memphis at Gadsden, the Black Barons won in spite of Memphis's Double Duty Radcliffe's homer and ten strikeouts from the mound, but the Red Sox finally ended their streak.

Returning to Rickwood for Independence Day, two shutouts over the Jacksonville Red Caps took the first half title. Then, barnstorming all the way to Winnipeg, Birmingham opposed St. Louis, the Clowns, and local clubs.

Satchel Paige faced the Black Barons in September in Oshkosh; rookie Grady McKinnis shut out the Monarchs as Birmingham tagged Paige for five runs to beat the lanky legend. Closing the season, Kansas City claimed the championship, while Birmingham finished second.

PERDUE ARRESTED

Former owner Frank Perdue was arrested in November 1940, charged with hiring a hitman for a contract murder. Following George McDowell's shooting, Perdue and McDowell's wife, Lillie, were implicated by the man who confessed to pulling the trigger, James Turner. Turner said that he shot McDowell for $200. Perdue and Lillie planned to cash out the victim's insurance, according to the *Birmingham Post*, which said that Frank Perdue supplied the weapon.

At the widely publicized trial, in exchange for life imprisonment instead of the death penalty, Turner testified openly about shooting George McDowell for Lillie and Perdue. As he was led from the courtroom, a handcuffed James Turner bolted from the bailiff and dove through a sixth-story window, plunging to his death. Lillie was acquitted, but Frank Perdue was found guilty and sentenced to ten years in the state penitentiary.

1942: Wartime Barnstorming

Birmingham opened camp with Dan Bankhead leading the pitching staff. Stars Lester Lockett, Tommy Sampson, and Goose Tatum were back, and veteran Ted Radcliffe brought his brother Alex to the team. Opening day welcomed Jacksonville to Rickwood Field, and nearly ten thousand fans came through the turnstiles. Birmingham defeated manager Jabbo Andrews's Red Caps.

In an April game against Homestead, Birmingham's Tommy Sampson lifted a deep fly ball into the outfield. Grays centerfielder David Whatley backed up and…it bounced off his head! Right fielder Sam Bankhead played the carom, gloving the ball midair for the out.

Birmingham spent weeks on the road, playing a home series to show off their new barnstorming partner before leaving again. New players were brought in; others were going out the door. Lester Lockett was drafted, and ace Dan Bankhead was in manager Welch's doghouse for being out of shape, eventually sent to Saperstein's Clowns.

Mobile native brothers Ted and Alex Radcliffe, pictured with Habana Leones, combined for nineteen All-Star appearances. *Dr. Layton Revel/Negro Southern League Museum.*

When Birmingham split a series with Jacksonville, they handed the first half flag to the Monarchs, just percentage points ahead in the standings. The Black Barons then barnstormed the Midwest. With a twelve-game winning streak on the line, Memphis ended the string, shutting Birmingham out. From there the Black Barons headed east to take on foes such as the Homestead Grays, Baltimore Elite Giants, Philly Stars, Black Yankees, and others.

They beat the legendary white-bewhiskered House of David team at Benton Harbor, but while traveling in Michigan, the team bus was wrecked, forcing a rare cancelation. Thankfully no players were injured.

The team bus was then totaled a few weeks later on the way to Indianapolis. Several players were injured when the bus overturned, but none seriously, although the team was forced to travel by train.

Manager Winfield Welch enjoyed "Welch Day," honoring him on September 20. Owner Hayes also gifted his players half the Rickwood gate proceeds before Birmingham again went on a barnstorming trip. Coming home, the club defeated the Clowns, and Dan Bankhead left for Army service following the game, the eighth former Black Baron in military service.

Birmingham finished second in the final standings.

1943: The Black Barons Hit the Road, World Series or Bust!

Manager Winfield Welch returned, and his club brought back much of its roster. Exhibitions with the Monarchs pitted Birmingham against Satchel Paige several times. On April 28, Paige worked three shutout innings against Birmingham in Montgomery. The next day, Satchel pitched five innings against them in New Orleans, allowing just two hits. May 2 at Rickwood was "Satchel Paige Day," and ten thousand fans turned out. The Black Barons gifted their former star a war bond and a loss, driving him from the hill in the sixth inning.

Opening day was in Cincinnati, and the clubs divided a pair of extra-inning games and then split two more in Memphis. The Black Barons finally came home to open the Rickwood schedule against Memphis, winning both ends of the doubleheader with more than twelve thousand in attendance.

TODAY
IS
"SATCHEL" PAIGE DAY at
Rickwood Field
DOUBLE-HEADER — THE FIRST GAME TO START AT 2 O'CLOCK
BLACK BARONS
VS.
KANSAS CITY MONARCHS
Winners of last season's American League pennant race and all the Inter-League Colored World Series.
"Satchel" Paige Pitches Today's First Game

Left: Ad for 1943 Satchel Paige Day at Rickwood Field. *Author's collection.*

Below: The 1940 Panama City Blue Sox, with manager Charlie "Two Sides" Wesley (*fifth from right*). *Author's collection.*

The Cincinnati Clowns, managed by Bunny Downs, visited and lost three times, including a 13–0 thrashing. Birmingham then ran a win streak to seven games, capped by Al Gipson striking out fifteen Black Crackers.

Weeks were spent on the road and rails. The Black Barons reportedly ran the table during the trip, winning every game. At Kansas City, they again battered Satchel Paige and then defeated the Cuban Stars at Chicago's Wrigley Field. They beat Chicago at Rickwood to open July, snaring the first-half championship and hitting the road again. Birmingham barnstormed from Atlanta to Winnipeg. Wrigley Field, Comiskey Park, Crosley Field, Forbes Field, white teams, local teams, touring teams, Cubans, Clowns, Black Yankees, and Red Caps—the Black Barons handled them all.

One highlight came at Chicago's Wrigley Field in a four-team doubleheader tribute to Satchel Paige's twentieth pro year. Twenty-five thousand fans watched Birmingham again beat the Cubans at Wrigley.

On August 21, Alvin Gipson struck out twenty Philly Stars, winning 5–1 and setting the club record.

Birmingham hosted other teams while the Black Barons were barnstorming, including the popular Panama City (Florida) Tigers. The Tigers, led by manager Two Sides Wesley, had many Birmingham-connected players.

Playoff Performance Propels BBBs to World Series Berth

The Black Barons were playoff-bound, facing Chicago in a five-city series that moved south for the final contests. After a dramatic series, the final game at Rickwood was an epic clash between longtime rivals. Black Barons hurler John Huber was phenomenal, facing just one hitter over

The 1943 Homestead Grays. *Back, from left to right*: Edsall Walker, James "Cool Papa" Bell, Roy Partlow, Thad Christopher, Josh Gibson, Johnny Wright, Ray Brown, Ernest "Spoon" Carter, Buck Leonard, and Candy Jim Taylor (manager). *Front, from left to right*: Jud Wilson, Jerry Bingham, Joe Spencer, Vic Harris, Sam Bankhead, and Matt Carlisle. *Public domain.*

the minimum and shutting out the Giants. The Black Barons were Negro American League champions.

Griffith Stadium in Washington, D.C., hosted the first game of the World Series. The Black Barons faced the star-studded Homestead Grays, managed by Candy Jim Taylor.

Birmingham's Alfred Saylor's five-hitter won game one. In game two, the Black Barons let a lead slip away in the ninth inning, eventually resulting in a tie, costing Birmingham a precious victory when the extra-inning game ended with midnight curfew.

Game three in Washington was a crushing eleventh-inning loss for Birmingham, who chose to pitch around Josh Gibson. With the bases loaded, Cool Papa Bell drove home the winning run to even the series.

In Chicago, Homestead shut them out in game four, 9–0. Josh Gibson slugged a grand slam, but Birmingham edged the Grays 11–10 in game five to even the series. In Indianapolis, the Grays again shut out Birmingham to move to the brink of a championship.

At Rickwood Field, the Black Barons battled scoreless until the eleventh inning, when Birmingham's Ed Steele knocked in the winning run and pushed the series to a final deciding game.

THE BIGGEST GAME: BLACK BARONS VS. HOMESTEAD GRAYS WORLD SERIES

In October 1943, Montgomery's Cramton Bowl hosted the deciding contest between the Birmingham Black Barons and the Homestead Grays. More than four thousand fans were on hand to watch the final game of the 1943 Negro League World Series.

For the Homestead Grays, led by manager Candy Jim Taylor, the outfield was anchored by Cool Papa Bell. Former Montgomery Grey Sox infielder Howard Easterling was at second base, alongside nine-time All-Star shortstop Sam Bankhead. Pitching for Homestead was Johnny Wright, who had just sealed the pitching triple crown, leading the league in wins, strikeouts, and earned run average.

The Black Barons were well stocked with talent of their own. Behind the plate was legendary catcher "Double Duty" Radcliffe. Shortstop Piper Davis was a six-time All-Star. An experienced outfield of Lester Lockett, Clyde Spearman, and slugger Ed Steele patrolled the grass.

Catcher Paul Hardy was available off the bench, and veteran pitcher Alfred Saylor got the start.

After falling behind 4–2 early, Homestead launched an eighth-inning rally, giving the Grays a come-from-behind victory. Four errors and nine men left on base doomed Birmingham's pennant hopes. Homestead reliever and future Hall of Famer Ray Brown earned the W, closing out the ninth inning to preserve the win.

Eight of Homestead's nine starters had base hits, and no Grays batter struck out. First baseman Buck Leonard had two hits, including a double and run scored. Leonard's first-inning single drove in Cool Papa Bell with the game's first run. Howard Easterling tied the game with an eighth-inning single that scored Buck Leonard and Josh Gibson. Then Sam Bankhead was clutch, driving in two more runs to give the Homestead Grays the lead.

Hall of Fame legend Josh Gibson had three hits, including a ninth-inning RBI double. He scored twice under the Cramton Bowl lights to lead his Homestead Grays to an 8–4 victory and claim the World Series championship.

Josh Gibson of the Homestead Grays. *Robert H. McNeill Family Collection, Library of Congress, Prints & Photographs Division.*

POSTSEASON CONTROVERSY

A New Orleans game in the championship series was canceled; instead, two exhibitions with Homestead were held at Rickwood, where Birmingham manager Winfield Welch was heard to say that the series wasn't supposed to have ended in Montgomery. Welch said that New Orleans was intended to be the final game, but after Montgomery promoters called their exhibition contest the "deciding game" on the AP wire, team owners agreed to let it stand. That drew angry responses from sportswriters, who questioned the wisdom of allowing exhibitions during the World Series. League officials stated that the series played out as planned, and Win Welch hastily denied the quotes attributed to him.

1944: BBBs Bounce Back Better, Double Duty Handles Double Shutouts at Yankee Stadium

Birmingham's roster was familiar: Double Duty Radcliffe, Ed Steele, Lester Lockett, Piper Davis, and Tommy Sampson were among the many returnees. The season opened in Chicago; Lester Lockett drove in seven as Birmingham won twice in a doubleheader. They then beat Chicago in Dayton and manhandled the St. Louis Stars in Knoxville.

When Rickwood Field hosted the home opener in mid-May, the large crowd of eleven thousand saw Birmingham win another doubleheader, dispatching the Monarchs by turning five double plays. The opening day crowd was bolstered by two school bands and uniformed American Legionnaires for the pregame flag raising ceremonies. However, midway through the ascent of Old Glory, the bugler confused everyone by playing taps instead of "The Star-Spangled Banner."

Left: Ted "Double Duty" Radcliffe with the Homestead Grays. *Robert H. McNeill Family Collection, Library of Congress, Prints & Photographs Division.*

Below: White teams were often part of the Black Barons' barnstorming tours. The *Buffalo News* touted the white Niagara Falls team hosting the Black Barons in 1944.

Opposite: Satchel's demands for more money to participate in the All-Star Game sparked changes in pay for the event. *Los Angeles Times Photographic Collection, UCLA Library Digital Collections.*

BASEBALL
TOMORROW NIGHT
AT OFFERMANN STADIUM—8:30 P. M.
BIRMINGHAM BLACK BARONS
Champions of Negro American League
VS.
NIAGARA FALLS DAYS
Strongest white team in Buffalo and Western New York, with Eugene "Huck" Geary in its line-up.

With a left-handed heavy batting order and strong pitching rotation, the Black Barons were a formidable challenge for all opponents. Rain mercifully halted the game against the white, semipro Niagara Falls Days after seven innings, with Birmingham ahead 9–0.

Birmingham defeated two teams in one day at Yankee Stadium on June 5, crushing the Philadelphia Stars and Black Yankees in a doubleheader double shutout. Twelve thousand fans watched Al Gipson and Dan Bankhead's stingy pitching, allowing just five hits combined. Bankhead struck out fourteen in the seven-inning second game. Ed Steele hit a towering 430-foot home run as Birmingham tallied thirty hits and twenty-two unanswered runs to sweep the doubleheader. Double Duty Radcliffe caught both games.

The Black Barons barnstormed widely across the Northeast and then to Texas. They visited Atlanta and came away first-half champs; then they faced Cleveland as part of a month-long July tour. One of the few home dates was a loss to the Monarchs' Satchel Paige, who tossed a four-hit shutout.

Six Black Barons were selected for the annual East-West All-Star Game at Comiskey Park, as well as manager Winfield Welch. Double Duty Radcliffe

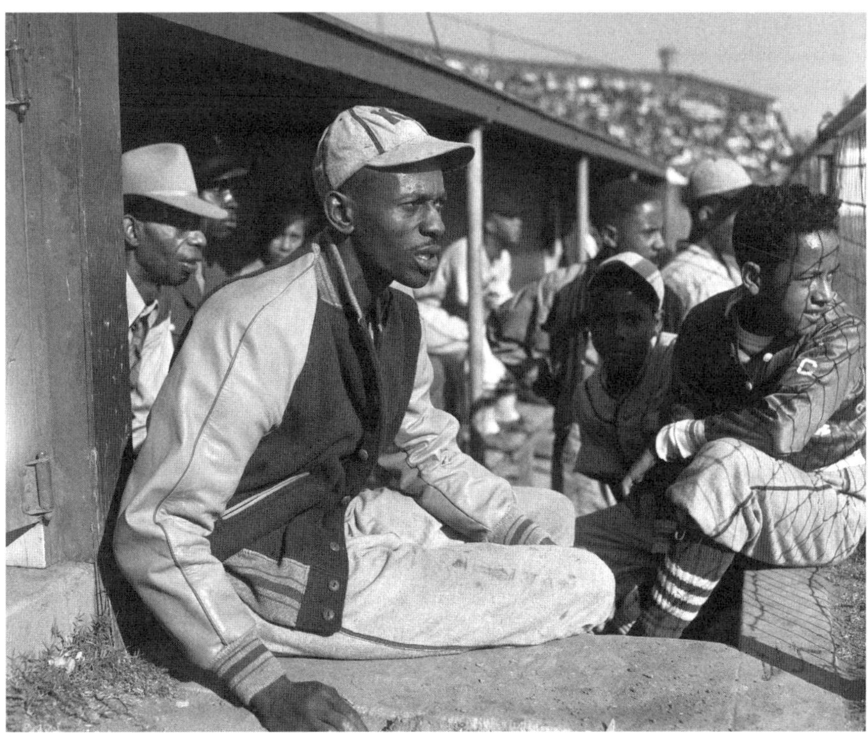

homered, and pitcher Verdell Mathis earned the win. Just hours before the game, both All-Star squads held out for more money, forcing league officials to give players a minimum of $100, up from $25. The flap started when Satchel Paige demanded 10 percent of the gate to participate and was replaced on the All-Star roster.

Satchel Pitches for Birmingham

In September, the Black Barons beat the Clowns in a doubleheader at Wrigley Field in game two. The *Chicago Tribune* reported that Satchel Paige pitched the first four innings for Birmingham, allowing three runs on five hits. Reports say that Satchel heard "tremendous and consecutive boos" during the game, the worst he had ever experienced, after his recent truancy from Chicago's All-Star Game.

Black Barons Earn World Series Rematch

The league's new stat service reported that Birmingham had a sparkling .298 batting average. Declared winner of both halves, the Black Barons were back in the World Series. So, too, was Homestead. The series opened at Rickwood Field.

Birmingham faced a brutal setback before the series. On the way back from a late-season game, a carful of players was hit head-on by a drunk driver. Slugger Tommy Sampson, who was driving, was left in critical condition. Three others were injured, all lucky to have survived the horrific crash.

With their stars in the hospital, the Black Barons were clubbed by the Grays. Josh Gibson and Buck Leonard each homered at Rickwood in the first game to win. Homestead then took game two with a late rally. Game three was nearly historic as the Black Barons managed just a single hit and were shut out. Facing elimination, Birmingham's Jim Huber tossed a three-hit shutout and won at Forbes Field in Pittsburgh.

The next day at Griffith Stadium, Homestead wrapped up the series with a 4–2 victory to earn the World Series title, again denying Birmingham the crown. The two clubs then played in New York and Philadelphia; the Grays won just for good measure.

BASEBALL TONIGHT
Third Game of Negro World Series
at
Rickwood Field
BLACK BARONS
vs.
WASHINGTON HOMESTEAD GRAYS
Game Starts 8:15

Above: Advertisement for the 1944 Negro World Series at Rickwood Field in the *Birmingham News*.

Right: Walter "Buck" Leonard with the Homestead Grays. *Robert H. McNeill Family Collection, Library of Congress, Prints & Photographs Division.*

In October, the Black Barons beat Augie Galen's white team at Oakland's Seals Stadium on a western tour. Following the tour, Sam Bankhead joined Roy Campanella and several other Alabama stars for winter ball in the Caribbean. Tubby Scales, Sam Jethroe, Terris McDuffie, John Markham, and others were All-Stars in the Dominican league.

1945: Bham's Barnstorming Days

Tommy Sampson was still recovering, but many regulars were back in Black Barons uniforms. Double Duty Radcliffe and Pepper Bassett were among the stars in the batting order. Opening day brought Cleveland to Rickwood, where the ceremonies went smoother, but the bugler again played taps. The

Buckeyes won the opener, and Birmingham took the nightcap and then split a pair in Montgomery before setting out on the road.

On April 23, fans at Montgomery's Cramton Bowl witnessed a classic pitching duel between the Black Barons and NY Cubans. Cuban starter Luis "Lefty" Tiant Sr. matched Birmingham's Fay Washington inning for inning, each pitcher allowing just one hit. With the game tied at two and two outs in the bottom of the ninth, a passed ball allowed the winning run to score, and the Black Barons won 3–2, giving Tiant and the Cubans the loss.

A doubleheader at Comiskey Park earned Birmingham two wins over Chicago. Jim Newberry's six-hit shutout in game one was followed by pitchers Willie Young and John Markham winning in game two. Willie Young, born with only one hand, was a veteran of the Birmingham Industrial League.

Birmingham pitcher Jimmy Newberry allowed a home run at the Polo Grounds, breaking his string of thirty-eight consecutive scoreless innings. Fourteen thousand fans attended the doubleheader against the NY Cubans.

On May 28, the Clowns were in Montgomery to face Birmingham for a league game. The Clowns scored in five of the first six innings for a 12–4 victory over the Black Barons, who sent three pitchers to the showers before the game was over. Former Montgomery Grey Sox Johnny Ray hit a homer under the lights at Cramton Bowl for the Clowns. This game illustrated the ability the Clowns displayed when the games were being counted toward the league schedule.

The following day, the Black Barons returned the favor, besting the Clowns, 6–1, behind Jim Newberry, who allowed just one unearned run in nine innings.

The Black Barons enjoyed their home away from home at Cramton Bowl, using their almost-home field advantage to beat the Monarchs on June 4 behind Al Saylor. Then, one month later on July 2, Birmingham's Saylor was victorious again, winning over the Memphis Red Sox and contributing at the plate with a double. July 4 was spent in Memphis, splitting a doubleheader with the Red Sox to end the first half in third place.

Later that month, the Black Barons played in Battle Creek, Michigan. They also played at Lafayette, Indiana, on the same night. When the cities found out that Birmingham was "two-timing" them, they withheld the proceeds from the games, totaling more than $700.

The Black Barons' string of Cramton Bowl victories was snapped by the New York Black Yankees on the evening of July 30. Yanks hurler "Neck" Stanley allowed just one run, and Birmingham made four errors to lose 4–1 in Montgomery.

The 1940s Memphis Red Sox jersey worn by Neil Robinson. *Public domain image courtesy of Collection of the Smithsonian National Museum of African American History and Culture.*

On August 20, the Black Barons wrapped their Montgomery schedule, defeating the Buckeyes, 8–4. Decatur, Alabama native Alonzo Boone was the winning pitcher for Birmingham, supported by Pepper Bassett's two doubles.

Griffith Stadium in Washington, D.C., was home to the Homestead Grays and Washington Senators. *Robert H. McNeill Family Collection, Library of Congress, Prints & Photographs Division.*

SATCHEL PITCHES FOR BIRMINGHAM (AGAIN)

An August appearance as part of a four-team doubleheader briefly reunited Birmingham and Satchel at Griffith Stadium. Originally scheduled first, last-minute shuffling left the Black Barons watching the Monarchs get beaten by Philadelphia in the opener. Paige, who also thought that his Monarchs played the nightcap, arrived late and instead pitched for Birmingham. Satchel tossed three scoreless innings, striking out six of Josh Gibson's Homestead Grays.

The Black Barons hosted Cleveland, winning the series, but the recently healed Tommy Sampson got spiked. Piper Davis was suspended for breaking an umpire's nose.

At the Polo Grounds in September, the Black Barons beat the Homestead Grays in the first game of a doubleheader and then beat the Cuban Stars in the nightcap with fifteen thousand fans in the stands. The late-season trip provided a positive end to the season but was too little too late, as Birmingham finished fifth of six.

CHAPTER 16

1946 BBBs STEP BACK FROM SAP

Winfield Welch abruptly resigned as owner Tom Hayes broke from promoter Abe Saperstein. Veteran Tommy Sampson was named manager. The Black Barons camp had plenty of prospects, many fresh from military service. Stars Lester Lockett and Jimmy Newberry were re-signed, but several players held out for $500 monthly salaries. The season opened in Cleveland against the league champion Buckeyes. The Black Barons split the two games on opening day and then lost in Toledo. Rickwood's home opener against Cleveland was a night game. More than seven thousand watched pitcher Jehosie Heard down the Buckeyes. Birmingham took three straight before Cleveland won the final game.

Without Saperstein bookings, the team played fewer dates, didn't stray as far from home, and largely stuck with familiar partners. Games against Montgomery's Red Sox were held in Jackson (Mississippi), Montgomery, Birmingham, Atlanta, and Gadsden.

The 1946 Black Barons versus Chicago American Giants, advertisement in the *Birmingham Weekly Review*.

The Black Barons barnstormed Texas and the Midwest. Facing Chicago, they reeled off a five-game win streak. Memphis dealt them a pair of losses to put a stop to the skein. Buck O'Neil had four hits at Rickwood on Independence Day to lead KC to a 15–1 win.

The 1946 Birmingham Black Barons. *Back, from left to right*: unidentified, Herman Bell, Emanuel Sampson, unidentified, William Powell, Lester Lockett, and Piper Davis. *Middle, from left to right*: unidentified, unidentified, Curtis Hollingsworth, John Britton, Artie Wilson, and Nat Pollard. *Front, from left to right*: unidentified, unidentified, unidentified, and Lee Moody. *Memphis and Shelby County Room, Memphis Public Libraries.*

The Fourth of July series went to the Monarchs, and the first half ended with Birmingham in second place.

Four team doubleheaders at Shibe Park in Philadelphia and New York's Polo Grounds pitted them against the Stars and Cubans. An August doubleheader against Chicago was split, followed by a visit from the Clowns. A series against Memphis wound up the season with the Black Barons landing well out of contention.

1947: A Hot Start in the New Bus

Many longtime Black Barons returned, among them Piper Davis, Ed Steele, and Pepper Bassett. Several newcomers were from the Industrial Leagues. Tommy Sampson returned to manage, and Tom Hayes purchased the team a brand-new, motor-in-the-rear bus. The club left to train in Florida but spent the first day working out at Alabama State University when the new bus broke down in Montgomery. After a busy spring ranging from Florida

Top: The 1947 Birmingham Black Barons. *Back, from left to right*: Pepper Bassett, Sam Williams, Jimmy Newberry, Herman Bell, Ed Steele, Piper Davis, William Powell, and Joe Scott. *Front, from left to right*: Jehosie Heard, Lee Moody, Alonzo Perry, Earl Ashby, Norman Robinson, Artie Wilson, John Britton, Curtis Hollingsworth, and Orinthal Anderson. *Memphis and Shelby County Room, Memphis Public Libraries.*

Bottom: The Birmingham Black Barons' new engine-in-the-back bus and driver. *Memphis and Shelby County Room, Memphis Public Libraries.*

to Oklahoma, the season began in mid-May. Opening the regular season in Cleveland with a loss, they then grabbed back-to-back wins.

However, following the hot start in Cleveland, the new bus caught fire. A woman drove behind the flaming bus honking her horn for more than half an hour before the players noticed her or the billowing smoke. Two games were canceled, some uniforms were destroyed, and the team was left stranded.

Back in Birmingham against the rival Monarchs, the Black Barons sent seven thousand fans home happy with a 5–2 win in the home opener. Then came the Clowns, Giants, Buckeyes, and Red Sox in home games followed by two-week tours. The Red Sox provided a soft landing for the road-weary Black Barons, who won series at home and in Memphis.

At the end of June, Birmingham handed three losses to league-leading Cleveland. The two clubs tangled in road games, landing in Ohio. They split a July 4 doubleheader, and Birmingham hit the road. After hosting a local exhibition game, they faced the Monarchs in Kansas City, the Eagles in Newark, and the Philly Stars in New York's Yankee Stadium. August began with a homestand sweep of Indianapolis at Rickwood.

Black Barons at Cramton

The Black Barons hosted six games in Montgomery, starting with a preseason exhibition against the Cleveland Buckeyes. The Black Barons fell 11–10 and then faced the Chicago Giants on June 2, scoring eleven runs to win easily.

On June 30, the Cleveland Buckeyes pitcher Clyde Williams allowed just two runs to beat Birmingham. Three weeks later, the Black Barons topped the Memphis Red Sox at Cramton Bowl, 7–4, on August 19. The Black Barons met Cleveland again on August 27, and the Buckeyes easily took the night game 10–4 over Birmingham.

On September 3, the Black Barons wound up their Montgomery appearances with an 8–5 victory over Memphis. Birmingham pitcher Sam Williams of Ketona, Alabama, out-dueled Memphis moundsman Spoon Carter of Harpersville, Alabama.

Several Black Barons were selected as All-Stars, including Piper Davis, who had three hits for the winning squad. Manager Tommy Samson quit when owner Hayes fined him for missing time while hospitalized with appendicitis.

"Smilin' Sam" Williams of Ketona, Alabama, signed with the Black Barons in 1947 for $300 per year. *Memphis and Shelby County Room, Memphis Public Libraries.*

Two thousand fans in Knoxville held their breath when Birmingham's John Britton hit a ninth-inning fly ball that struck the top of the fence, bouncing high in the air before falling over the wall for a game-winning home run to defeat the Clowns in a late-season game.

Birmingham landed in third place but was much improved at the turnstiles.

CHAPTER 17

THE MAYS DAYS

1948

Training at Montgomery's Alabama State University's Athletic Field, manager Piper Davis's team played their always-busy preseason schedule.

Opening at home against Cleveland, the Black Barons split a doubleheader and then barnstormed to Ohio, where Birmingham hooked up with the Clowns. Much touring ensued, with the Black Barons enjoying success against league foes. The club moved to the top of the standings, largely on Pepper Bassett's .444 batting average.

Birmingham's Black Barons continued to host games at Cramton Bowl. On Thursday, April 22, more than two thousand fans enjoyed an exhibition between the Black Barons and Indianapolis Clowns that featured thirty combined hits. The Clowns emerged victorious, 13–9.

The Black Barons hosted four league games at Cramton Bowl this season, starting with Cleveland's Buckeyes on May 3. The Buckeyes shellacked the Black Barons, 15–3, posting twenty hits and aided by six Birmingham miscues. Attendance for Montgomery's first Monday night game of the regular season was listed at three thousand.

On June 19, Birmingham fell to Chicago, 2–1, at Cramton Bowl. About ten days later, on June 30, the Black Barons were again beaten, this time by the Clowns, losing 9–2. The Black Barons got back in the win column on August 7, beating Cleveland, 4–3, behind starter Alonzo Perry, who struck out nine Buckeyes and allowed just one run.

The 1948 Black Barons pitching staff. *Back, from left to right*: Sam Williams, Alonzo Perry, and Bill Powell. *Front, from left to right*: Nat Pollard, Jehosie Heard, Jim Newberry, and Bill Greason. *Memphis and Shelby County Room, Memphis Public Libraries.*

The Black Barons branched out across Alabama in 1948, playing series in Tuscaloosa's Alberta Park, Dothan's Wiregrass Stadium, and one-game stops in Huntsville's Lincoln Park and Decatur's Legion Field.

Enter Willie Mays

During a Sunday doubleheader at Rickwood, a young outfielder made his Birmingham debut. Willie Mays had arrived, batting eighth and taking a walk in two at-bats in a late June win over Indianapolis.

Birmingham easily nabbed the first half title while downing Memphis in a July 4 doubleheader. Mays played the first game, going hitless but making four putouts in left field. The players divvied a $500 bonus for the first half championship.

While they were barnstorming widely against top opponents—including Newark, Cleveland, and the NY Cubans—centerfielder Norm Robinson's broken ankle led manager Piper Davis to insert Willie Mays into Birmingham's everyday lineup.

Mays had three hits, with a double and a triple, and stole a base in an August loss to the Monarchs in KC. Willie had a game-winning double to beat Cleveland in Memphis.

Facing the Buckeyes at Alberta Park in Tuscaloosa on August 13, in the second inning against Chet Brewer, Willie Mays hit his first home run over the left field wall. That homer isn't counted among Willie's career numbers because no box score was published, only game reports.

When Birmingham came home to face the Cubans, Willie was now batting fifth. In Lexington, Willie Mays hit a three-run homer to beat the Cubans at Blue Grass Field. Again, no box score was publicized.

The Monarchs' second-half title set up a playoff series. Willie Mays had a huge postseason; he won the first game with an eleventh-inning walk-off RBI single. In game two, Mays had three hits, a clutch RBI, and a run scored. After the Monarchs evened the set with three wins, pitcher Bill Greason put Birmingham in the World Series with a four-hit effort, defeating the Monarchs, 5–1.

Black Barons outfielder Willie Mays. *Memphis and Shelby County Room, Memphis Public Libraries.*

World Series Rematch with Homestead

Homestead's Grays took three games easily before Birmingham's Willie Mays drove home a dramatic ninth-inning run to win game four. Homestead

Five Homestead Grays: Dan Wilson, Luis Márquez, Matt "Lick" Carlisle, Sam Bankhead, and Walter "Buck" Leonard. *Robert H. McNeill Family Collection, Library of Congress, Prints & Photographs Division.*

won the series three days later in New Orleans. It would be the final Negro League World Series. Following the season, Jackie's All-Stars beat the Black Barons in an exhibition that featured Jackie Robinson knocking a double and a triple and stealing home at Rickwood Field.

1949: Willie's World

The Negro National League folded as teams struggled following the integration of MLB. Interest cratered as fans turned their attention to major-league games. The Black Barons, in the Negro American League, began radio broadcasts for the first time and played in new uniforms purchased for the previous World Series.

Piper Davis piloted spring drills at Alabama State University. Willie Mays was back with the team but still attending high school, playing only home games until graduation. Bill Greason, Jimmy Newberry, and Joe Scott were among the returnees.

The Birmingham Black Barons of 1948. Willie Mays is seated at front left. *Memphis and Shelby County Room, Memphis Public Libraries.*

This unidentified first baseman with the Black Barons is likely Joe Scott or Cain Burgess. *Memphis and Shelby County Room, Memphis Public Libraries.*

Opening day at Rickwood was a Black Barons victory over Cleveland, with Willie Mays wearing no. 5. The club played well at home with Mays but struggled on the road without him. There was no replacing Willie Mays.

Barnstorming ensued, and stops include New York's Polo Grounds, Philadelphia, Pittsburgh, Virginia, Kentucky, and all points between. With school finished, Mays began destroying league pitching, reported as batting .420 through the start of June. On June 4, in a doubleheader against the Cubans at the Polo Grounds, Willie Mays hit a homer in the ninth inning of the first game, his first in New York.

Pitcher Jimmy Newberry broke his arm, and the team began bringing in new players, including "Spoon" Carter. Birmingham threatened in the first half but landed in second place. It was announced that Black Barons games would be televised for the first time. Sunday, July 3, against Memphis was the first broadcast.

Independence Day featured three games, a Rickwood doubleheader followed by a night game in Tuscaloosa. Any diamond within two hundred miles of Birmingham was a potential venue, and sportswriter Marion E.

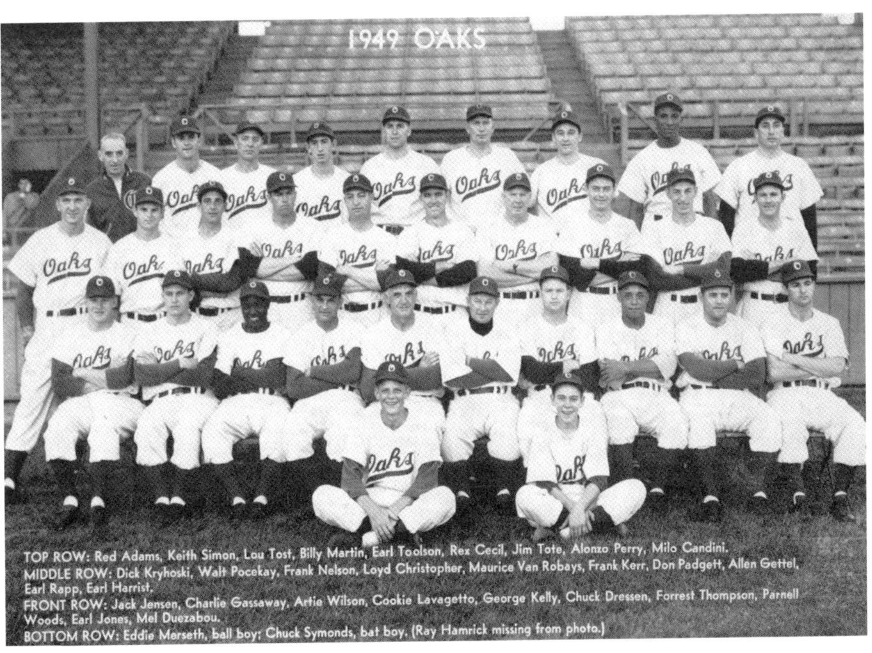

The Oakland Oaks' 1949 team included former Black Barons Alonzo Perry, Artie Wilson, and Parnell Woods. *Author's collection.*

BASE BALL

OUR POWERFUL

Birmingham Black Barons

vs

DIXIE LAND'S POPULAR

New Orleans Creoles

(Featuring the Only Woman In Professional Baseball)
Something None of Us Have Seen Before

AT THE

MISS TONI STONE
Second Sacker

Alberta Park

Friday Sept. 9

At 8:00 P.M.

Admissions

ADULTS: $1.00
CHILDREN . . 50c

A 1949 advertisement for the game between the Birmingham Black Barons and the New Orleans Creoles with Toni Stone in Tuscaloosa. *Author's collection.*

Jackson said that some towns "couldn't be found on a relief map, but the crowds were consistent with many played to in larger cities."

On July 9, Willie Mays stole two bases and drove in two runs to beat Memphis. The next night, he had five hits and a game-winning RBI over Philly as he continued his torrid pace. On the twenty-seventh, he downed Memphis with a game-winning RBI in the ninth inning, his fourth hit of the contest.

On July 30, Jimmy Newberry returned, but the team struggled to contend. Alonzo Perry was sold to Oakland, where he joined two other former Black Barons, Artie Wilson and Parnell Woods. Then manager Piper Davis was signed by the Boston Red Sox. Piper led the league in batting, and fans were not surprised by the move.

EPIC BOWL BATTLE FEATURES A-MAYS-ING THROW

On Wednesday, August 24, the Black Barons and Kansas City Monarchs faced off at Montgomery's Cramton Bowl. The long-standing rivals expected a good game, but neither likely anticipated the lengthy contest to come.

The Black Barons scored in the first inning; the Monarchs pushed a run across the plate in the third frame to tie the game. The Monarchs scored again in the fifth, and Birmingham answered in the bottom half of the sixth, tying the game again.

That's when Black Barons starter Bill Powell decided to bear down. Powell started racking up strikeouts and refused to let the Monarchs score again. Not to be outdone, Monarchs hurler Jim LaMarque matched Powell inning after inning.

In the seventh inning, with the score tied at two, a Monarchs batter drove a deep fly ball off of Cramton Bowl's centerfield wall. Black Barons outfielder Willie Mays turned, raced to the 387-foot mark on the fence, picked the ball up on one hop as it rebounded off the wall, and made a spectacular throw that did not bounce before reaching the third baseman. The tag was easily applied to the startled runner, ending the Monarchs' scoring threat.

The game remained tied through nine innings. Both pitchers continued across the tenth, eleventh, and twelfth innings. Herman Bell replaced Birmingham's reliable catcher Pepper Bassett due to exhaustion. They went scoreless in the thirteenth inning, and when the fourteenth frame passed, the game was still knotted. Both pitchers had tossed more than seven scoreless innings, and fourteen overall, but neither was accepting any relief. In the top of the fifteenth inning, the Monarchs were again turned away, one-two-three, by Black Barons hurler Billy Powell.

When the Black Barons came to bat in the bottom of the sixteenth, light-hitting backup catcher Bell singled to open the inning. After a weak single moved him to second, the pudgy Bell scrambled home with the winning run when pitcher Billy Powell slapped a game-winning hit into the outfield. After three hours and fifteen minutes, the Black Barons won 3–2.

Birmingham starter Bill Powell went the distance, striking out nine and driving in the winning run. However, what fans were buzzing about was Willie Mays's amazing throw.

September exhibitions pitted the Black Barons against the New Orleans Creoles and female infielder Toni Stone in Tuscaloosa and Decatur. Willie Mays hit a 350-foot homer over the Rickwood wall to down Cleveland on September 23. Birmingham's Spoon Carter struck out nine.

The Black Barons hosted three September exhibition games at Montgomery, beginning on September 20 against Cleveland. Black Barons starter Bill Greason outpitched Buckeye hurler George Jefferson, and Birmingham won 3–2 in front of more than 1,500 fans. About one week later, on September 28, the Memphis Red Sox beat the BBBs, 11–1, at the Bowl but fell to the Black Barons the next day, 4–5.

The series against Memphis included games at Montgomery's Cramton Bowl and Alabama State University's Athletic Field, but as Birmingham fell in the standings, they stopped sending reports. The Black Barons wound up the season against Indianapolis, landing in fourth place.

The Jackie Robinson All-Stars were Birmingham's postseason exhibition partners. The Black Barons beat Jackie, 3–1, in Talladega and then lost to Don Newcomb at Rickwood with more than fifteen thousand fans watching. Willie went oh-fer.

1950: Black Barons Burn Through Another Bus

Vic Harris was hired to manage, and many veterans returned, as well as Willie Mays, who now wore no. 21. The home opener against Memphis attracted four thousand fans, but Birmingham dropped the game. Piper Davis returned after being let go by Boston, helping Birmingham to a nice early season winning streak.

Things started to go bad when another bus was wrecked on the way to New York. The fire destroyed their gear, uniforms, and transportation, and they were beaten by the Cubans at the Polo Grounds. Pitching ace Jimmy Newberry jumped the team. Then, on June 22, Willie Mays was signed by the New York Giants. In August, the Chicago Giants' three white players weren't allowed to play at Rickwood. Police required them to sit in the white section of the grandstand in street clothes.

Kansas City was awarded the first half erroneously due to a statistical error that omitted Birmingham games. The Black Barons fell to third place as the Monarchs won both halves to claim the championship. The Birmingham Black Barons would continue as a franchise until 1962, when the Negro American League disbanded.

CHAPTER 18

AFTER JACKIE

After Jackie Robinson toured with the KC Monarchs and then joined the Dodgers, Black baseball fell from the sports pages almost overnight. Three top Montgomery teams—the Montgomery Dodgers, the Montgomery Tigers, and the Montgomery Giants—occupied league spots but got little notice. The Dodgers disappeared after two seasons, the Giants lasted three or four, and only the Montgomery Tigers were still active after 1951.

1946: Montgomery Red Sox/Dodgers

The NSL reorganized following World War II, and Montgomery's Red Sox entered in the loop's third season, but the same reporting issues prevailed.

First announced as the Montgomery Dodgers by team president Jake Whatley, the name was changed to Red Sox in June. Some speculated that the Brooklyn Dodgers objected, but there is no proof to support the hypothesis. More likely, the addition of several former Memphis Red Sox players sparked the change. The Dodgers/Red Sox were a farm club for the Birmingham Black Barons, according to Emory O. Jackson, who called them the "little Black Barons" in his *Atlanta Daily World* column and said the team was spurred by the addition of lights to the ASU athletic field.

Four players on the Dodgers/Red Sox infield were former Homestead Grays, including shortstop Norman "Jelly" Jackson, third baseman Ray

Battle, Rob Robertson, and James Davis. Former Alabama State football star Carvin Crowe was the catcher for the club.

The Montgomery Red Sox shuffled managers often, first skippered by "Spoon" Carter, followed by John Jackson, then swiftly by Buck Fielder, and finally Earnest Robinson. Among the players were Montgomery native Jim Canada and infielder Buck Fielder. Henry Newberry was the Sox top pitcher; other hurlers included Laymon Ramsey and James Bolden. In June, Red Sox pitcher Henry Newberry faced his brother Jimmy, pitching with the Black Barons.

Montgomery's Red Sox made a lengthy trip to New York, facing the Atlanta Black Crackers at the famous Polo Grounds in late June, falling 14–6. Montgomery and the Atlanta Black Crackers barnstormed through northern cities such as New York, Brooklyn, Baltimore, and others. The Montgomery Red Sox traveled in style with their own touring bus.

In New York, the Montgomery club was off its game badly, with one reporter saying that the club "tossed the ball around in scandalous fashion, booted ground balls, dropped pop flies, to say nothing of the bases on balls." The report continued, noting that Montgomery "employs a top-notch press agent" for their pregame hype, but after giving up fourteen runs, the Red Sox would not be asked back.

Reuben Jones managed the Red Sox until June 1947, when he was reported as leading a Black Barons farm club called the Texas Rangers. Playing in Florida, Jones's Rangers claimed to be the '46 Texas Negro League champs, but there was no TNL that year.

1947–1949: Montgomery Giants and Tigers Lead Local Pack

The '47 Montgomery Black Giants were reportedly undefeated through late June behind teenage ace Lefty White and managed by catcher John Morgan. Slugger Joseph "Sky" Blue led the batting charge. Facing clubs such as the Kilby Prison Tigers, the Tuskegee Tigers All-Stars, the Selma Black Cloverleafs, and Alabama State, the Giants also made road trips to Enterprise, Pensacola (Florida), and Columbus (Georgia).

Opposite: The Montgomery Tigers' felt uniform patch. *Author's collection.*

Above: The Mobile Black Shippers, circa 1940s, from the *Weekly Review of Mobile, Alabama. Author's collection.*

Here's a sample Montgomery Giants lineup from a July game against rival Tuskegee: Bell in right field, Rozell Cofield in left, Barnette in centerfield, George "Smoke Ball" Edwards at shortstop, Oscar Joseph handling the keystone sack with Jack Mitchell at first base, George Young patrolling the hot corner, and catcher John Morgan receiving the pitches from Williams. Another Giants pitcher, Willie "Black Dizzie" Dean, was said to be catching the eye of scouts.

In 1948, the Montgomery Giants hosted the visiting New Orleans Creoles, with female centerfielder Essie Wilson. The Giants, a force in the Montgomery City League, would join the newly reorganized Negro Southern League thanks in part to their appearances against teams like the Creoles.

In 1949, the Montgomery Tigers faced the New Orleans Creoles, now with female infielder Toni Stone. The Creoles also played other teams in Montgomery, facing Shreveport's Tigers and the Birmingham Blues at ASU's Hornet Stadium.

1949's Montgomery Tigers were the last Montgomery team in the Negro Southern League. David "Slaughter" Shaughter represented the club at the Negro Southern League meeting. A shell of its former self, this incarnation of the NSL included the Mobile Shippers, the Pensacola Gulls, the Nashville Cubs, the Gadsen Florida Tigers, and the Atlanta Brown Crackers. As always, stats and standings were sporadic and incomplete. The league would fold within two years.

CHAPTER 19

FADING AWAY

With the arrival of television, MLB integration, and other factors, the market for Negro League baseball crumbled nationwide. Black baseball in Alabama, however, remained strong. Teams were formed, games were played, and leagues were organized as the sport went back to its nineteenth-century roots. Amateur and semipro clubs played in nearly every cotton field, cow pasture, and empty lot in the state.

Northern barnstorming teams appeared in smaller towns as well as bigger cities but struggled to draw fans. Popular games were again the ones featured at picnics, fairs, and church events, between local clubs or competing businesses. It was a homecoming for the game, back in the hands of those who played simply for enjoyment.

Whether it was the Daphne Tigers, the Bay Minette Scouts, the Mobile Buckeyes, the Opp Blue Jackets, the Lockhart Braves, the Gadsden Brown Derbys, the Tallassee Black Indians, the Muscle Shoals Redbirds, the Brewton Black Cats, the Uniontown Black Steers, Bessemer's Wenonah Star Back club, or even the Scottsboro Flying Saucers or the Attala Atom Bombs, there was baseball everywhere.

Willie Mays made his MLB debut in 1951, but he was not alone. Many Black Alabamians enjoyed major-league success. Greats such as Billy Williams, Hank Aaron, Monte Irvin, Willie McCovey and others became fixtures on Major League Baseball All-Star teams and entered Cooperstown's Hall of Fame. Later, their Negro League counterparts would also be recognized and enshrined.

Left: Two young Tuskegee baseball players, circa 1940s. *Estate of Willy M. Jackson.*

Below: The Tuskegee Veterans Hospital team. Willy Jackson is second from the right. *Estate of Willy M. Jackson.*

Birmingham's annual throwback game at Rickwood Field, with its iconic scoreboard in 2019. *Author's photo.*

Baseball arrived, thrived, and evolved in Alabama. Overcoming challenges, dangers, and oppression, Black Alabamians faced what was thrown at them and excelled in the sport as players, executives, journalists, officials, and fans. Their contributions to the game are simply immeasurable, and their stories are a vital part of the American experience.

SELECTED BIBLIOGRAPHY

Adelson, Bruce. *Brushing Back Jim Crow*. University Press of Virginia, 1999.

Brown, Charles A. "Reconstruction Legislators in Alabama." *Negro History Bulletin* 26, no. 6 (1963). Association for the Study of African American Life and History.

Brunson, James. *Black Baseball, 1858–1900: A Comprehensive Record of the Teams, Players, Managers, Owners and Umpires*. McFarland & Company, 2019.

Burgos, Adrian, Jr. *Cuban Star: How One Negro League Owner Changed the Face of Baseball*. Hill & Wang, 2011.

Irvin, Monte, and Phil Pope. *Few and Chosen Negro Leagues: Defining Negro League Greatness*. Triumph Books, 2007.

Plott, William. *Black Baseball's Last Team Standing: The Birmingham Black Barons, 1919–1962*. McFarland & Company, 2019.

———. *Negro Southern League: A Baseball History, 1920–1951*. McFarland & Company, 2015.

Ribowsky, Mark. *Complete History of the Negro Leagues*. Kensington Publishing Corporation, 1998.

Riley, James. *The Biographical Encyclopedia of the Negro Baseball Leagues*. Carroll & Graff Publishers, 1994.

Spalding, Albert. *Spalding's Official Baseball Guide*. Horton Publishing Company, 1888.

Watkins, Clarence. *Baseball in Birmingham*. Arcadia Publishing, 2010.

———. *Baseball in Montgomery*. Arcadia Publishing, 2017.

White, Sol. *Sol White's Base Ball Guide*. Camden House, 1984.

Unpublished

Plott, William J. Interviews with Former Grey Sox players, 1994–2006.
Revel, Dr. Layton, and Luis Munoz. "Forgotten Heroes: John Beckwith." Center for Negro Leagues Baseball Research, 2014.

Newspapers

Alabama Beacon.
Albany-Decatur Daily.
Anniston Star.
Athens Post.
Atlanta Constitution.
Atlanta Daily World.
Baltimore Afro-American.
Birmingham News.
Birmingham Post-Herald.
Birmingham Reporter.
Birmingham Weekly Review.
Buffalo News.
Bulletin Index (Pittsburgh, PA).
The Call.
Canebrake Herald.
Chattanooga Times.
Chicago Defender.
Chicago Tribune.
Cincinnati Enquirer.
Columbia Breeze.
Columbus Ledger.
Coosa River News.
Daily Mountain Eagle.
Daily State Sentinel (Montgomery).
Davenport Daily Times (Minnesota).
Elba Clipper.
Eufaula Daily Times.
Freeman News.
Ft. Payne Journal.
Greenville Advocate.
Independent American (Troy, AL).
Indianapolis Freeman.
Kingsport (TN) Times.
L.A. Times.
Luverne Journal.
Macon Telegraph.
Marengo News.
McLure's Magazine (1905).
Memphis Avalanche.
Montgomery Advertiser.
Montgomery Journal.
Montgomery Times.
Nashville Banner.
Nashville Globe.
Nashville Tennessean.
New Orleans Times-Picayune.
New York Age.
New York Clipper.
Our Mountain Home.
Ozark Banner-Register.
Pensacola News.
Pensacola Times.
Piedmont Inquirer.
Piedmont Post.
Pittsburgh Courier.
Prattville Progress.
Roanoke Leader.
Scottsboro News.
Selma Times.
Sporting Life.

Sporting News.
St. Louis Argus.
Titusville Herald.
Troy Messenger.
Tuscaloosa News.
Tuskegee News.
Union Springs Herald.
Voice of the People (Birmingham, AL).
Weekly Review of Mobile, Alabama (1942).

Internet

alasu.edu.
archive.org.
baseballhall.org.
baseball-reference.com.
cnlbr.org.
drmiraculous.blogspot.com.
floridamemory.com.
net54baseball.com.
newspapers.com.
retrosheet.org.
seamheads.com.

ABOUT THE AUTHOR

Shane Earnest, creator of the award-winning *The Montgomery Baseball Blog* under the name "Dr. Miraculous," has built a reputation for revealing the hidden stories of Alabama baseball. Telling the tale of baseball in Alabama is his lifelong passion. For nearly two decades, he has covered a variety of baseball action, working as an on-field photographer and researching the origins of the game. A lifelong resident of Montgomery, Alabama, he has interviewed hundreds of current and former players, officials, and front office executives dating back to the 1920s, including MLB All-Stars and Hall of Famers. Recognized as the leading source of Alabama baseball history on the web, Shane combines gonzo-style journalism and a love of local lore to cast new light on stories long buried. Shane works as a freelance photographer and musician, as well as lecturing on baseball history and writing his popular blog. He lives in Montgomery with his wife and a few happy cats.